The Index of Global Philanthropy and Remittances 2010

D1307516

HUDSON INSTITUTE
CENTER FOR GLOBAL PROSPERITY

The Center for Global Prosperity (CGP) provides a platform—through conferences, discussions, publications, and media appearances—to create awareness among U.S. and international opinion leaders, as well as the general public, about the central role of the private sector, both for-profit and not-for-profit, in the creation of economic growth and prosperity in the developing world.

The CGP's core product is the annual *Index of Global Philanthropy and Remittances*, which details the sources and magnitude of private giving to the developing world. The *Index* reframes the discussion about the roles of the public and private sectors in foreign aid by showing that the full scale of a country's generosity is measured not just by government aid but by private giving as well.

The CGP supports free societies, including capital markets, the rule of law, government transparency, free trade and press, human rights, and private property— prerequisites for economic health and well-being.

PARTNERS & SUPPORTERS

Achelis Foundation
Bristol-Myers Squibb Foundation
Centre d'Etude et de Recherche sur la Philanthropie
Charities Aid Foundation
Charles Sellen, Independent Researcher
Chevron Foundation
Committee Encouraging Corporate Philanthropy
Foundation Center
GuideStar Data Services
Instituto per la Ricerca Sociale
Institute of International Education
John Templeton Foundation
Leonard & Tobee Kaplan, Toleo Foundation
Merck & Co.
Partnership for Quality Medical Donations
Patrick M. Byrne, Chairman & CEO of Overstock.com
Social & Economic Sciences Research Center, Washington State University
Stein Brothers AB, Research Consultancy
The Case Foundation
The CHEAR Foundation
The Lynde and Harry Bradley Foundation
The Urban Institute Center on Nonprofits and Philanthropy
Western Union Foundation
Dr. Wiepking, VU University Amsterdam Department of Philanthropy

ADVISORY BOARD

Dr. Peter Ackerman
Dr. George B.N. Ayittey
Dr. Arthur Brooks
Ernest Darkoh, M.D.
Dr. William Easterly
Mary Jo Jacobi-Jephson
Mamadou Koulibaly
Dr. Deepak Lal

Alain Madelin
Dr. Allan H. Meltzer
Dr. Susan Raymond
Dr. Michael P. Ryan
Ruth Wedgwood, J.D.
Rosa Whitaker
Amb. Richard Williamson
Amb. R. James Woolsey

Publisher
HUDSON INSTITUTE

Director
DR. CAROL C. ADELMAN

Deputy Director
HEIDI METCALF LITTLE

Editor
PATRICIA MILLER

Senior Fellow
JEREMIAH NORRIS

Research Fellow
YULYA SPANTCHAK

Executive Assistant
KACIE MARANO

Design and Art Direction
DAVID HERBICK DESIGN

Interns
HAEIN LIM
CHARITY-JOY ACCHIARDO
ANDREW BALTES
PATRICK BROWNE
JASON FARRELL
ZIVILE GEDRIMAITE
EMILY GIKOW
ANNA GREENE
ZENAH HASAN
EIMEAR O'LEARY-BARRETT
AI GHEE ONG
PETER J. TELAROLI
YAN ZHANG

The CENTER for
GLOBAL
PROSPERITY

CENTER FOR
GLOBAL PROSPERITY

HUDSON INSTITUTE
1015 15th Street, NW
Sixth Floor
Washington, DC 20005

Phone: 202-974-2400
Fax: 202-974-2410
www.global-prosperity.org

ISBN: 978-1-55813-169-9

ISSN: 1946-7885

© 2010 Hudson Institute

Philanthropy to the developing world remained steady in 2008 despite the global recession and dire forecasts. Remittances continued to grow in the same year as well. Our predictions for 2009 in last year's *Index of Global Philanthropy and Remittances* held true, as U.S. individual giving and global remittances declined less than expected (by single digits only). Philanthropy and remittances provided a much needed lifeline to poor people throughout the world. And they were more resilient to the downturn than private capital.

As economies around the world struggled through 2008 and 2009, private capital flows from developed to developing countries fell dramatically—from $325 billion in 2007 to $121 billion in 2008. Short-term capital (bank lending and bond purchases) constituted the majority of this decline. The good news is that foreign direct investment (FDI), the more important long-term capital expenditure, decreased by only $11 billion (from $189 to 178 billion). FDI from the United States to developing countries actually increased to $54 billion. And, as the global economy showed signs of recovery in late 2009, even short-term capital flows began to pick up.

Among the highlights of the Center for Global Prosperity (CGP) and our fifth annual *Index* are:

- Global philanthropy, remittances, and private capital investment accounted for 75% of the developed world's economic dealings with developing countries.
- Government aid increased to its highest levels in 2008 as donor countries responded to the global recession; even with this increased aid and the dramatic decline in private capital flows, government aid accounted for only 25% of the developed world's total economic engagement with the developing world.
- Remittances actually grew in 2008, although at a slower rate than 2007; they are expected to decline in 2009 by only 6%.
- CGP is pleased to feature new writers who share their views on growth and prosperity in developing countries; we are moving into exciting new areas such as harnessing the power of diaspora and indigenous philanthropy as well as the growth of impact investing in emerging economies.
- CGP's new blog provides up-to-date commentary on global trends and issues, and our new biweekly *Blog Brief* summarizes the most important blogs and debates on global philanthropy, remittances, and development.

Through CGPs work over the last five years, we have helped change the global conversation on foreign assistance. By measuring private flows from developed to developing countries, we have shown that these flows greatly exceed government aid. In addition, we have showcased new private players, explaining how many are delivering assistance more efficiently than government aid. As a result, smart government aid agencies increasingly are launching creative and successful public–private partnerships.

CGP's research has provided the empirical foundation for scholars, governments, charities, and development aid practitioners to adapt their own work to the changing foreign aid architecture. We now have 12 distinguished research partners, all working to improve and refine global philanthropy and remittances numbers. We look forward to expanding these partnerships and creating an international network to promote generosity by measuring, comparing, and publicizing philanthropy to and in developing countries. All four editions of the *Index* have been widely featured in major media outlets, as well as academic journals and government reports. The February 2010 ForeignAffairs.com, in "What to Read on Foreign Aid" featured the *Index* as "a one-stop compendium of the best available data on global philanthropy."

In 2009 we distributed more than 3,000 copies of the *Index* and had over 8,000 downloads from our web site, www.global-prosperity.org. Our 10,000 monthly web site hits and radio interviews reaching over 29 million listeners in 2009 indicate the large and growing interest in private giving.

As the *Index* distribution and impact grows, we are learning more about our readers. They reflect a mix of nonprofits, researchers, policymakers, corporations, and individual donors. They use the *Index* for writing and presentations, to decide what projects to support, to develop more workable overseas projects, and to learn about best practices. Over half found the *Index* "very useful" to their work and used all sections of the *Index*—from the trends, charts and tables, to case studies and the remittances section.

We thank our readers and supporters for your continued involvement in this important endeavor. Above all, we thank the incredible people and organizations featured in all of our *Indexes* for their generosity, as they work hand-in-hand with gifted partners in the developing world. We believe that measuring and publicizing this private giving will improve it through growth and better practices.

DR. CAROL C. ADELMAN
Director, Center for Global Prosperity
Hudson Institute

Resilience in Tough Times

The Haitian earthquake prompted an outpouring of private philanthropy around the world. In Thailand, the Lions club, Buddy group and the Red Cross of Thailand organized an elephant parade through the streets of Bangkok to raise money from tourists and business owners for Haiti quake victims.

As in all sectors of the economy across the world, the recession that officially began in 2008 has had a broad impact on international philanthropy, decreasing some flows while highlighting the importance of more resilient flows. The recession has also caused individuals and institutions to be more creative in their giving and is bringing about innovation that may help wring some

of the inefficiencies out of traditional giving models.

As a result of the recession, private capital flows from developed to developing countries fell from $325 billion in 2007 to $121 billion in 2008, which undoubtedly had a major impact on developing countries' economies. However, foreign direct investment (FDI), the segment of private capital flows that has the most long-term impact on emerging economies, was the least affected of the four flows that comprise private capital flows to the developing world (FDI, private export credits, securities of multilateral agencies, and bilateral portfolio investment), falling from only $189 billion to $178 billion in 2008.[1] There are also indications that the worst of the crisis has passed for developing countries and that private capital flows have already begun a recovery in the last three quarters of 2009 and beginning of 2010.

As private capital flows fell in 2008, private philanthropic flows and remittances remained some of the most important sources of funding for much of the developing world. Even though individuals and institutions in the developed world faced recession in 2008, their private giving, through philanthropy and remittances, once again outpaced government spending. Private philanthropy and remittances from the developed to the developing world were $233 billion compared to government aid of $121 billion. As predicted in last year's *Index*, remittances from all countries to developing countries have remained a remarkably resilient economic flow during the global recession. Remittances to developing countries continued to rise in 2008, slowing only in the last quarter. They totaled $338 billion in 2008, a 17% increase from 2007 and almost three times the total in 2002.[2] Of the $338 billion, $181 billion comes from the developed nations.

As the response to the January 2009 earthquake in Haiti illustrated, global generosity seems to know no bounds. Americans alone gave $774 million dollars within the first five weeks of the earthquake.[3] The generous response was also faster than ever thanks to text messaging technology, which allowed the Red Cross to raise an unprecedented $32 million in $10 donations sent via text message.[4] Money poured into the Haitian relief effort from individuals, governments and corporations around the world. Seven-year-old Charlie Simpson from Fulham, England, used JustGiving. com to attract sponsors for his five-mile charity bike ride around his neighborhood and single-handedly raised more than $300,000 for the Haitian relief effort.[5]

OFFICIAL DEVELOPMENT ASSISTANCE

Official development assistance (ODA) rose to $121 billion from all DAC donor nations in 2008, representing an increase of 11.7% over 2007.[6] The growth of ODA still does not keep pace with combined flows of private philanthropy and remittances. Government leaders and multilateral institutions are recognizing that the aid architecture has changed and philanthropy is a widely recognized resource in international development. More and more, we see that global leaders are encouraging public–private partnerships to leverage resources of their governments. U.S. Secretary of State Hillary Rodham Clinton acknowledged: "The problems we face today will not be solved by governments alone. It will be in partnerships—partnerships with philanthropy, with global business, partnerships with civil society."[7]

Clinton has outlined her vision for U.S. foreign aid that focuses on development activities that are "accountable, transparent and results-oriented."[8] This new vision, Clinton said, also includes working in closer partnership with developing countries in a bottom-up approach: "In the past, we have sometimes dictated solutions from afar, often missing our mark on the ground. Our new approach is to work in partnership with the people in developing countries by investing in evidence-based strategies with clear goals that the countries have taken the lead in designing and implementing."[9]

David Cameron, the leader of the Conservative Party in the United Kingdom, has pledged to maintain the country's commitment to ODA, but wants to give citizens a greater say in how it is spent. His MyAid plan will allow British citizens to determine how a portion of UK Government aid is distributed by voting on funding for 10 ongoing international development projects, with funding allocated in proportion to the number of votes received.[10]

2009 GIVING TRENDS

As expected based on previous recessions, there was a decline in overall philanthropy in 2009, but indications are that philanthropy from some sources may rebound in 2010. Some areas of philanthropy expect a more focused, strategic philanthropy sector to emerge as a result of cutbacks and consolidations.

According to a September 2009 survey by the Founda-

From Aid to Independence

BY MAMADOU KOULIBALY

Fifty years after independence, Africa remains a major concern of international policy. Development has stagnated in many places across the continent. The reasons are multifaceted. Property rights are not well defined; money is a state-owned tool used to accumulate budgetary deficits, and the family unit has been destroyed by poverty.

It is time to reevaluate African states and their policies. To establish a path to prosperity for its people, Africa needs to radically change its old practices and create new institutions and a new legal infrastructure to ensure a coherent framework for institutional reforms.

International aid plays a key role in the development outlook for Africa. While well-intentioned, development assistance for Africa has been less effective than it ought to be. Those who call for an increase in the volume of official development assistance overlook the fact that markets, not governments, drive prosperity. It is essential to move away from the idea that markets are good for developed countries while state-administered economies are better suited for poor African countries.

Official assistance, in fact, is often used by African states to promote centralized national development, even though the past century taught us that central planning and authoritarianism fails and that market economies and democracy work. Private assistance of the sort cited in the *Index of Global Philanthropy and Remittances* is far more effective, as it is voluntary and often person-to-person or market-based.

What poor African countries need to focus on is building states that are based on the rule of law. Currently national policy is centered on strong presidents that enjoy excessive discretionary power and lead weak states incapable of performing basic functions such as rendering justice and ensuring the security of their citizens. Businesses are inhibited in their operations and growth by poor legal frameworks and pervasive corruption that discourages saving and investment.

To this end, Africa needs to break from its current method of governing by institutionalizing the fundamental principles of an open society where liberty is central and in which every human being is empowered to act and make

> Poor African countries need to focus on building states that are based on the rule of law. State building needs to be based on respect for the individual, their freedom, rights and responsibilities.

decisions. The quality of human capital being the key lever of economic growth and prosperity calls for improved health, education and training services for African populations.

The lack of a functional banking system in Africa also continues to discourage investment. Less than three percent of the population in Africa has bank accounts. Banks do not know how to properly manage risk and as a result do not lend sufficient capital to small and medium-sized businesses to promote growth of this important segment; instead, they use their capital to finance state budgets.

To promote economic growth, Africa must remove corruption from its customs system and reduce customs tariffs and simplify its tax system. Fiscal controls need to be improved. Ownership of rural land must be clarified to assign property rights to rural landowners.

This will ensure the development of an active mortgage market to support rural development and poverty alleviation.

In short, the level and flow of aid dollars matter less than improving interstate relations in Africa, ending unfair trade practices, improving governance and ensuring property rights in poor countries. Farmers, often the largest social and professional class in African nations, are still among the poorest in Africa because they live off lands that are not governed by precise ownership rights.

Poor African countries need to focus on building states that are based on the rule of law. State building, in turn, needs to be based on respect for the individual, their freedom, rights and responsibilities. In the context of this approach to development, the state must be non-tribal and non-ethnic; responsible, limited and determined to maintain order; and working for the common interest.

Africa needs to generate bold new ideas to help rebuild the institutional foundations of its own development. My goal is to create a think tank to work with youth, civil society leaders and politicians to generate these ideas for francophone Africa and put us on the path to a new, truly independent, self-determined future.

Mamadou Koulibaly has been President of the National Assembly of Côte d'Ivoire since January 2001 and also serves on the Hudson Institute's Center for Global Prosperity advisory board.

Serving the "Missing Middle" in Africa
BY ROD MacALISTER

Many people agree that the best way to unleash Africa's long-term economic and social potential is from the bottom up. The hard part is figuring out how to do that. After years of investing in Africa with ConocoPhilips, including social investment, I had developed some good ideas about the use of investment to spur stability and prosperity in developing countries. I joined the U.S. African Development Foundation (ADF) as president and CEO in 2006. The ADF is a U.S. government agency that "invests" in small and medium enterprises, farmer cooperatives, and community groups in Africa to create jobs in poor communities. The mission of ADF to empower unbanked entrepreneurs was sound; however, the operation had flaws and missed many opportunities. It took ADF a

year or more to make a positive funding decision, which is intolerably slow for farmers captive to a growing season. And because ADF is mandated by Congress to serve the "poorest of the poor," it funded weaker entities and left the stronger ones to fend for themselves, on the theory that they could qualify for commercial finance. In Africa, however, banks do not lend to those without collateral, credit histories, audited accounts, and the ability to pay high interest rates over short periods. Most of all, I came to see the making of grants for economic purposes as harmful, since this taught recipients that money is free rather than having a market value, which weakened, rather than strengthened, the people seeking assistance.

Simple arithmetic reveals almost

unlimited scope for private sector funds to serve the so- called "middle of the pyramid." The OECD estimates that small and medium sized enterprises (SMEs) constitute some 70–80% of economic activity almost everywhere in the world. However, they are the least served businesses in Africa. Before the recession, it was estimated that there was up to $25 billion in capital seeking investment opportunities in Africa alone. The downturn has evaporated this capital for now but longer term there is no denying the vast potential for Africa to take its place in the mainstream global economy. Over the next 15 to 20 years, Africa will accomplish this with a blend of indigenous and non-African investment.

Co-founder Jon Halverson and I created the Africa Middle Market Fund

tion Center, 2009 foundation giving was projected to decrease by more than ten percent from 2008, which is in line with its earlier projections of an 8–13% decline in foundation giving.[11] Foundations are also predicting that the decline in giving will last through 2010, reflecting steep losses in their assets in 2008 and the need to spread these losses over a three to five year period. Just over a quarter of respondents expected to decrease giving in 2010, while 50% expected to hold giving steady in 2010 with 17% planning to increase giving.[12] The good news is that nearly 80% of respondents to the survey expect the field of philanthropy to become more strategic and creative in the future as a result of the economic crisis, putting a greater emphasis on sustainability, collaboration and transparency.[13]

Two thirds of respondents to the Foundation Center survey said they have reduced their operating expenses to ensure giving levels.[14] For instance, despite having entered the recession with a highly liquid portfolio, The Ford Foundation's assets fell 30% to $9.5 billion. In response, the Ford Foundation closed international offices[15] and cut $22 million in costs, but will increase its payout rate in 2009 and 2010 to 6.5% to honor its grant commitments.[16, 17] Because of efforts like these, foundation giving rose by an estimated 2.8% in

2008 despite a drop in assets of nearly 22%.[18]

Corporate philanthropy was also expected to feel the effects of the recession in 2009. A February 2009 survey of 158 companies by the Conference Board found that 45% were reducing giving in 2009 and 16% were considering cuts in giving.[19] Yet, many companies were projecting robust giving programs in 2009. Corporate philanthropic leaders from IBM and General Mills projected an increase in giving in 2009, and GE and Moody's said their giving would stay the same as 2008.[20] Giving increased slightly in 2009 for Coca-Cola, MetLife and Wal-Mart's corporate foundations. Both Verizon and Bank of America said giving was steady in 2009.[21]

Other corporate leaders said they were going to increase volunteerism and other forms of non-cash giving to offset flat or declining funding. IBM was planning to expand its pro bono consulting program and Moody's recently has started an employee volunteerism program that gives employees an afternoon off to volunteer with local charities.[22] Corporate giving is expected to begin recovering in 2010. According to a survey of major Chicago companies in late 2009, 65% planned to maintain or increase giving in 2010.[23]

A spate of mergers and acquisitions in the pharmaceutical industry, including Pfizer's acquisition of Wyeth, as a vehicle for individuals and institutions to invest in and serve mid-size companies in Africa for both profit and social impact (blended value). Once fully capitalized at an estimated $50 million, the fund will make loans and equity investments in firms that need between $500,000 and $2 million—above the needs of microfinance and below those of corporations. SMEs financed by the Africa Middle Market Fund will be companies that can grow 25–50% a year for five years. Investees will be required to employ international financial and business management standards to maximize success. We seek "Africans serving Africans"—growing their local economies. The sectors of focus for the fund are agriculture (food, livestock feed and biofuels) and energy infrastructure.

There are a number of similar funds operating in this space in developing countries. The Small Enterprise Assistance Funds (SEAF) is a well known entity established since 1989 and currently working in more than 30 countries. SEAF is a blended organization with both public and private institutions that has made 250 investments. Horizon Equity has made more than 40 private equity investments in Africa, mainly in South Africa, with the majority of investments returning at least five times the cost. SpringHill Equity Partners is another example of a social private equity company that is supporting SMEs in Africa. They are concentrated in Southern and East Africa and yield 10–20% in annual financial returns. Root Capital is a nonprofit organization that invests in SMEs. Established 10 years ago they have provided over $150 million in credit to 255 businesses in 30 countries with a 99% repayment rate from borrowers and 100% repayment to investors.

There are a number of challenges to establishing this kind of fund. Investments in SMEs are high risk, complex and offer a very wide range of returns. Negative perceptions of Africa persist. The time and cost to establish a fund like the African Middle Market Fund and get it capitalized are huge barriers to entry. The African Middle Market Fund opened for investment in October of 2008, just as the worldwide economy plunged, leaving many potential investors too short of capital to invest. There are also regulatory challenges, as blended value funds cannot afford to pay full tax rates so they fall into a gray area in most tax codes that distinguish only between for-profit and nonprofit entities.

That said, the upside potential in Africa is vast. Between the quality and quantity of SMEs, the rising middle class (some 400 million), huge areas of un- and under-cultivated arable land, undeveloped minerals, rapidly improving technological capabilities and reforming governments, the top countries in Africa are poised to take their place among the hot economies in the next 10 years.

Rod MacAlister is managing director of the Africa Middle Market Fund, a new private fund targeting investments in SMEs in East Africa. MacAlister previously served as president of the United States African Development Foundation.

Roche's acquisition of Genentech, and Merck's acquisition of Schering-Plough, may affect giving patterns in this key philanthropic area. According to Lori Warrens, executive director of the Partnership for Quality Medical Donations, industry consolidation will result in the merging of medical donation programs and missions, potentially changing the direction and volume of current medical donation efforts.[24]

The recession may well push corporations towards more strategic charitable activities that favor sustainable growth and profitability.[25] Both "green" strategies that benefit the environment and fair trade programs are examples of value-based programs that can benefit bottom lines in tough times. An A.T. Kearney study of 99 companies in 18 industries from May through November 2008 found that in 16 out of 18 industries, companies committed to environmental sustainability outperformed industry financial averages by 15% over the 6 months studied.[26]

According to the Fairtrade Foundation, worldwide Fairtrade sales witnessed a 22% increase in 2008 over 2007, amounting to $4 billion despite the recession.[27] A survey of 25,000 UK households found average fair trade purchases increased 5.5%.[28] Cadbury recently converted its Dairy Milk chocolate bars to Fairtrade and plans to quadruple the amount of Fairtrade cocoa it gets from Ghana from 5,000 to 20,000 tons.[29] In 2009, Starbucks doubled the amount of Fairtrade coffee it imports to the United States and Sam's Club quadrupled its purchases of Fairtrade bananas.[30]

Individual giving remains a bright spot in private philanthropy, with only a modest decline projected for 2009. In February 2010, Boston College's Center on Wealth and Philanthropy projected that U.S. household charitable giving for 2009 will total between $216 and $218 billion, representing a decline of between 4.8% to 5.7% from 2008. The center's preliminary projections for 2010 suggest that total household charitable giving could return to the pre-recession (2007) level of $234 billion, in the best-case scenario, or decline at most an additional 3.9% from 2009 estimates.[31]

Many charities saw a surge of donations late in 2009 that boosted their 2009 fundraising totals to near their targets. Catholic Charities saw a 21% surge in donations in December 2009 that put it within its $7.1 million goal for the year. A third of nonprofits surveyed by the *Chronicle of Philanthropy* in December 2009 said their donations were higher in December than they had been the previous year and one-half polled in January said donations rose over the holiday season compared to 2008. Online giving portal GlobalGiving.org reported that donations were 67% higher in December 2009 compared to December 2008.[32]

GLOBAL INNOVATION AND COLLABORATION

The recession has been an opportunity for some international organizations to diversify their donor base, expand their fundraising globally, and capitalize on the wealth of individuals and foundations outside the United States. A recent study found that high net-worth philanthropists living in Asia donate the highest proportion of their wealth to charity compared to their peers, giving more than 12% of their wealth to charity compared to 8% by North American and Middle Eastern high net worth individuals.[33] To capture this wealth for philanthropic purposes, World Vision has opened three new international fundraising offices since 2005 and now raises almost two-thirds of its annual budget outside the United States. In 2008, United Way Worldwide raised 28% of its budget outside the United States. Rotary International has recruited hundreds of Rotarians around the world to volunteer to raise money to support branch offices in Australia, India, and South Korea.[34]

The recession is also driving nonprofits to find new ways to operate that are more efficient and collaborative. A Bridgespan Group poll of 117 nonprofits found that 20% were contemplating a merger or acquisition to reduce costs and expand or enhance services. Similarly, a British study found that one in three UK charities were considering a merger or acquisition and one in six was considering joining a commercial organization to deal with financial strain.[35]

In March 2009, the International Trachoma Initiative, founded in part by Pfizer in 1998, and the Task Force for Child Survival and Development, a nonprofit public health organization founded by the World Health Organization, UNICEF, the United Nations Development Program, the World Bank, and the Rockefeller Foundation, merged to collaborate and expand their efforts to eliminate trachoma, the world's leading cause of preventable blindness.[36] In July 2008, the Renaissance Charitable Foundation acquired 95 funds totaling $35 million from the SEI Giving Fund, a donor advised fund designed to make charitable giving easier. This will mean more flexible giving standards and lower minimum donations for SEI donors.[37] In August 2008,

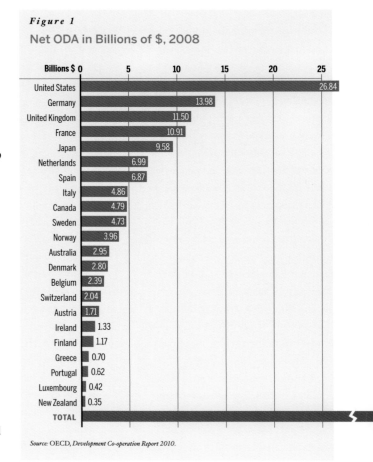

Figure 1

Net ODA in Billions of $, 2008

Billions $		
United States		26.84
Germany		13.98
United Kingdom		11.50
France		10.91
Japan		9.58
Netherlands		6.99
Spain		6.87
Italy		4.86
Canada		4.79
Sweden		4.73
Norway		3.96
Australia		2.95
Denmark		2.80
Belgium		2.39
Switzerland		2.04
Austria		1.71
Ireland		1.33
Finland		1.17
Greece		0.70
Portugal		0.62
Luxembourg		0.42
New Zealand		0.35
TOTAL		

Source: OECD, *Development Co-operation Report 2010.*

the British-based Harvest Help and Irish charity Self Help Development International merged to form Self Help Africa, reducing management and administrative costs to channel more money into aid programs.[38]

Technology also continues to bring innovations to charitable giving. As text messaging technology accelerated the pace of charitable responses to the Haitian earthquake, a proliferation of online tools is helping citizens be smarter about where to give. Charity Navigator, the largest of the charitable rating tools, is expanding its rating services to measure the effectiveness of charities. New entries into the online charity rating field include GiveWell, Philanthropedia, and GreatNonprofits. These new platforms are experimenting with crowdsourcing, assessment questionnaires and the distribution of investment-like research.[39]

Online donations also continue to grow in popularity in the United States. U.S. charities raised 26% more money online in 2008 than 2007, according to a new study. The average size of the donation decreased from $86 in 2007 to $71 in 2008, but the number of online donations increased 43%, suggesting nonprofits are adjusting to the recession by raising more small donations from a larger pool of donors. According to Marc Ruben, a vice president at M+R Strategic Services, which conducted the survey, "Online fund raising isn't seeing the same kinds of declines that other channels are."[40]

POTENTIAL BARRIERS TO INTERNATIONAL PHILANTHROPY

Not everything is faster and freer in the world of international philanthropy. The International Center for Not-for-Profit Law reports that in some countries, barriers to foreign philanthropy are on the rise just when more philanthropy is needed. "When there are economic difficulties, there's the rise of protectionism," said Douglas Rutzen, president of the center. "To a certain extent we're witnessing the rise of philanthropic protectionism."[41] For instance, Eritrean law restricts multi-lateral and bi-lateral agencies from funding any domestic PVOs. In 2008 Jordanian law requires PVOs to gain permission from the government prior to receiving foreign funding. A recent Ethiopian law prohibits PVOs whose revenues from a foreign source exceed 10% of its budget from participating in a variety of activities to promote human and democratic rights. In June 2008, Russia levied a 24% tax on all non-government approved foreign contributions to local PVOs.[42] Efforts are required within the international community to ensure that philanthropic protectionism does not hinder the growth of a vibrant private philanthropy sector.

Overall, however, as the success stories in this 2010 issue of the *Index of Global Philanthropy and Remittances* illustrate, international philanthropy remains a vibrant sector as international funders and local communities come together to find on-the-ground solutions to the world's most pressing problems.

TRENDS IN TOTAL GOVERNMENT AID TO DEVELOPING COUNTRIES

As the depth of the global recession became apparent, the international community became increasingly concerned that foreign aid to developing countries would drop. Analysis of previous recessions suggests that financial crises have a negative impact on aid flows.[43] In October of 2008, the Organisation for Economic Co-operation and Development (OECD) reached out to the Development Assistance Committee (DAC) donor nations' heads of state to stay committed to their 2010 aid pledges and DAC donors committed to not reducing their ODA levels.[44] In August of 2009, the Obama administration reiterated its promise to double foreign aid

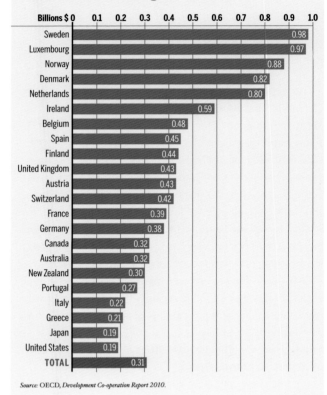

Figure 2

Net ODA as a Percentage of GNI, 2008

Billions $	
Sweden	0.98
Luxembourg	0.97
Norway	0.88
Denmark	0.82
Netherlands	0.80
Ireland	0.59
Belgium	0.48
Spain	0.45
Finland	0.44
United Kingdom	0.43
Austria	0.43
Switzerland	0.42
France	0.39
Germany	0.38
Canada	0.32
Australia	0.32
New Zealand	0.30
Portugal	0.27
Italy	0.22
Greece	0.21
Japan	0.19
United States	0.19
TOTAL	0.31

Source: OECD, *Development Co-operation Report 2010.*

over the next four years despite the recession.[45]

In 2008, as in previous years, the majority of DAC nations fell far short of reaching a 0.7% target set by some developed countries. Only five countries (Denmark, Luxembourg, Netherlands, Norway and Sweden) have formally committed to this target and reached it. Furthermore, a gap is widening between what DAC donors commit to and what they actually disburse. In 2008 that gap widened to nearly $22 billion from $7 billion in 2007.[46] In 2008, the DAC estimated that $30 billion was still needed to meet the 2010 requirements for aid.[47]

Total ODA for 2008 (the most recent available data) was a record level of $121 billion (Figure 1), which represents an 11.7% increase in real terms over the 2007 total of $103.5 billion.[48] The amount of debt relief grants remained largely unchanged from 2007, totaling $8.8 billion in 2008.[49] While in 2007, ODA as a percentage of GNI fell from 0.31% to 0.28%, in 2008 ODA flows reached the highest volume recorded to date and have returned to 0.31% of combined GNI (Figure 2).[50]

Austria and Norway were the only two nations that showed a drop in ODA, with a 12.4% and a 2.5% decrease in real terms, respectively.[51] Austria's drop was largely a result of a decrease in debt relief.[52] While both the United States and the United Kingdom increased their assistance by more than 20%, smaller nations such as Portugal, Spain and Greece also showed significant increases of 22% or more.[53]

As in 2007, in 2008 only five countries (Norway, Sweden, Denmark, Luxembourg and the Netherlands) exceeded the Monterrey target of allocating 0.7% of GNI to aid budgets. These nations' ODA amounted to $18.9 billion, or 16%, of total DAC assistance. The United States remains the largest contributor of ODA by volume, with $26.8 billion in 2008. Germany, the United Kingdom, France, and Japan follow and, with the United States, remain the top five contributors of ODA by volume in 2008. Total ODA for these five nations increased by $11 billion from 2007 to 2008 and amounted to $72.8 billion, or 60% percent, of total DAC assistance.

Africa was the region receiving the largest portion of aid, with a total of $44 billion in receipts.[54] Iraq and Afghanistan were once again the top recipients of aid in 2008 with flows amounting to $9.9 billion and $4.9 billion respectively.[55] The Middle East, excluding North Africa, received $19.8 billion or 16 percent of total ODA.

U.S. GOVERNMENT AID TO DEVELOPING COUNTRIES

As seen in Figure 1, total U.S. ODA was $26.8 billion in 2008, a 20.5% increase in real terms (accounting for both inflation and exchange rate movements) from 2007.[56] While this large increase did little to change the U.S. ranking in the ODA to GNI ratio, the U.S. remains by far the largest donor in absolute amounts of ODA. U.S. government aid was nearly twice the amount of the next highest donor, Germany. Moreover, 19% of Germany's ODA is due to debt relief, whereas it is only 1% of U.S. ODA.[57]

The increase in ODA from the United States occurred in all regions of the world. Least developed countries, which are the poorest developing countries, saw the largest increase in aid from the United States — 43.2% increase to $7 billion.[58] Regionally, United States aid to Africa rose the most by an estimated 43.5% to $6.7 billion.[59] Aid also rose to Asia by $1 billion, totaling $8.9 billion, and to the Americas by $0.5 billion, totaling $1.9 billion in 2008.[60] U.S. humanitarian aid rose significantly as well, from $3 billion in 2007 to $4.4 billion in 2008.[61] Of total humanitarian aid, $2.4 billion went to sub-Saharan Africa.[62]

U.S. TOTAL ENGAGEMENT WITH DEVELOPING COUNTRIES

The problem with judging countries' generosity and development impact by the measure of government aid alone is that

Table 1

U.S. Total Net Economic Engagement with Developing Countries, 2008

	Billions of $	%
OUTFLOWS		
U.S. Official Development Assistance	$26.8	17%
U.S. Private Philanthropy	$37.3	23%
Foundations	$4.3	12%
Corporations	$7.7	21%
Private and Voluntary Organizations	$11.8	32%
Volunteerism	$3.6	10%
Universities and Colleges	$1.7	5%
Religious Organizations	$8.2	22%
U.S. Remittances	$96.8	60%
Total Outflows	$160.9	100%
INFLOWS		
U.S. Private Capital Flows	$28.8	100%
Total Inflows	$28.8	100%
U.S. Total Net Economic Engagement	**$132.1**	

Sources: OECD; Hudson Institute's remittances calculations from DAC donors to DAC recipients based on data from the World Bank's Migration and Remittances Team, 2009; Hudson Institute, 2010.

the figure excludes the vast amounts of private giving from American foundations, corporations, private and voluntary organizations, universities and colleges, religious organizations and individuals sending money back to their home countries. A more complete way of measuring donor impact on the developing world is to look at a country's total economic engagement—including official flows, philanthropy, remittances, and private capital flows—with developing countries. Table 1 provides this more complete picture of American investment and generosity in the developing world.

The most apparent change from 2007 numbers is the significant decline in U.S. capital flows to developing countries. In 2007, these flows accounted for the largest portion of U.S. economic engagement, amounting to $97.5 billion in outflows, which was a 56% increase from the previous year. In 2008, private capital flows were hit so hard by the banking crisis and global recession that the United States received more inflows from developing countries than outflows, totaling $28.8 billion. For this reason, Table 1 above separates financial flows into outflows from the United States to developing countries and inflows into the United States from developing countries.

Foreign direct investment (FDI) and bilateral portfolio investment make up the majority of the U.S. private capital flows. Generally, private capital flows can be volatile from year to year, since FDI and bilateral portfolio investment are combined. FDI is the more stable flow, and it actually increased by nearly $10 billion to $54.2 billion in 2008 from $45.6 billion in 2007. Thus FDI, a relatively long-term investment, was not responsible for the drop in private capital in 2008. The decline in net capital flows can be attributed to a drop in bilateral portfolio investments (bank lending and bond purchases) which declined to negative $75.8 billion in 2008 from $59.8 billion in 2007. Not surprisingly, this occurred because of the banking crisis in 2008, and the general demand for liquidity resulted in many U.S. lenders pulling money out of developing nations. The negative value indicates that the private capital flows from developing countries into the United States were greater than outflows from the United States to developing countries in 2008.

Although bilateral portfolio investment took a big hit in 2008, philanthropy from the United States to developing countries—which includes contributions from foundations, corporations, private and voluntary organizations (PVOs), individual volunteers, religious organizations and colleges and universities—held steady at $37.3 billion compared to $36.9 billion in 2007, and exceeded official U.S. aid by more than $10 billion. As with last year, PVOs accounted for the largest portion of U.S. philanthropy going overseas at $11.8 billion.

Remittances from individuals, families, and hometown associations in the United States going to developing countries reached an estimated $96.8 billion in 2008, the largest outflow

> American citizens, through contributions of volunteer time and money, gave more to the developing world in 2008 than any other DAC donor gave in ODA alone. Total U.S. philanthropy at $37.3 billion represented nearly one third of all donors' ODA.

from the United States into developing countries. This is more than three and a half times larger than official U.S. government aid and 60% of the total U.S. outflows. In last year's Index, CGP predicted that remittances would remain resilient relative to private capital, and they have, underscoring their stability even during harsh economic conditions.

As some of the most steady and reliable flows to developing countries, philanthropy and remittances must be accurately measured and included when measuring all assistance flows. When ODA from the United States is measured as a percentage of GNI, the United States shares last place with Japan at 0.19%, as shown in Figure 2. If, however, private philanthropy and remittances are added to the equation, the United States ranks in sixth place out of the 22 donor countries. U.S. private assistance alone compares favorably to other DAC donor's ODA. For example, American citizens, through contributions of volunteer time and money to U.S. PVOs, gave more to the developing world in 2008 than any other DAC donor gave in ODA alone. Total U.S. philanthropy at $37.3 billion represented nearly one third of all donors' ODA.

ALL DONORS' ASSISTANCE TO DEVELOPING COUNTRIES

In *Index 2009*, we reported that in 2007 private capital flows were the largest portion of private flows to developing countries. In 2008, that story changed. Private capital flows were hard hit by the banking crisis in the U.S. and in other donor countries. These flows declined to $121 billion in 2008 from $325 billion in 2007. Although private capital flows declined, combined private flows were still higher than public flows from developed to developing countries.

As we see in Figure 3, together the three private financial flows—philanthropy, remittances, and private capital investment—from all donor countries amounted to $355 billion in 2008, almost three times larger than ODA alone. Figure 3 shows the magnitude of the difference between private and public flows to the developing world over the last 15 years. Seventy five percent of all DAC donors' total economic engagement with the developing world is through private financial flows. As in the past decade, remittances continue to exceed ODA and this year account for the majority of private flows.

In 2007, private capital flows accounted for the majority of all private flows and were three times the size of public flows.

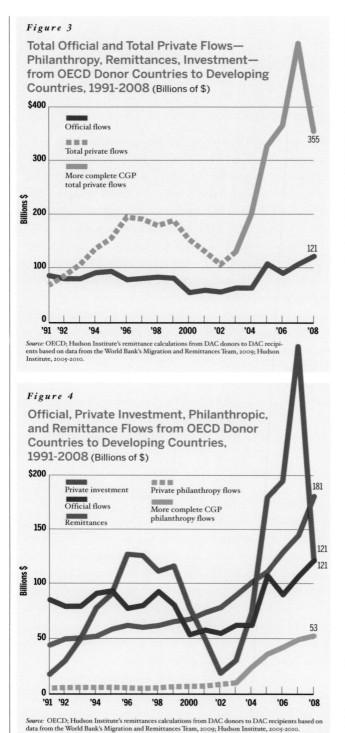

Figure 3

Total Official and Total Private Flows—
Philanthropy, Remittances, Investment—
from OECD Donor Countries to Developing
Countries, 1991-2008 (Billions of $)

- Official flows
- Total private flows
- More complete CGP total private flows

Source: OECD; Hudson Institute's remittance calculations from DAC donors to DAC recipients based on data from the World Bank's Migration and Remittances Team, 2009; Hudson Institute, 2005-2010.

Figure 4

Official, Private Investment, Philanthropic,
and Remittance Flows from OECD Donor
Countries to Developing Countries,
1991-2008 (Billions of $)

- Private investment
- Official flows
- Remittances
- Private philanthropy flows
- More complete CGP philanthropy flows

Source: OECD; Hudson Institute's remittances calculations from DAC donors to DAC recipients based on data from the World Bank's Migration and Remittances Team, 2009; Hudson Institute, 2005-2010.

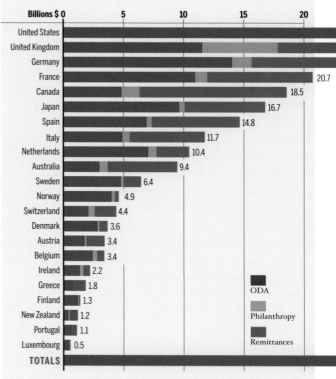

Figure 5

Total Asistance from OECD Donor Countries to
Developing Countries: ODA, Philanthropy and
Remittances, 2008 (Billions of $)

Country	Value
United States	
United Kingdom	
Germany	
France	20.7
Canada	18.5
Japan	16.7
Spain	14.8
Italy	11.7
Netherlands	10.4
Australia	9.4
Sweden	6.4
Norway	4.9
Switzerland	4.4
Denmark	3.6
Austria	3.4
Belgium	3.4
Ireland	2.2
Greece	1.8
Finland	1.3
New Zealand	1.2
Portugal	1.1
Luxembourg	0.5
TOTALS	

- ODA
- Philanthropy
- Remittances

Source: OECD, *Development Co-operation Report 2010*; Hudson Institute's remittance calculations from DAC donors to DAC recipients based on data from the World Bank's Migration and Remittance Team 2009; Stein Brothers, AB, Scandinavia 2009-2010; Charles Sellen, France, 2008-2009 and VU University Amsterdam Department of Philanthropy, Netherlands, 2009; Instituto per la Riceraca Sociale, Italy, 2009; Le Cercle de Cooperation des OND de Developpement, Annual Report, Luxenberg, 2009; Vrije Universiteit Amsterdam, Geven in Nederland 2009, Netherlands, 2009; Council on International Development, Annual Report, New Zealand, 2009; Plataforma Portuguesa das ONGD, Annual Report, Portugal, 2009; Coordinadora de ONG Para El Dessarrollo Espana, Informe de La Coordinadora de ONG Para El Desarrollo-Espana Sobre El Sector De Las ONGD, Spain, 2009; GuideStar Data Services, United Kingdom, 2009; Center for Global Prosperity, United States, 2009-2010.

In 2008, private capital flows dropped and became nearly identical to ODA. The main reason for this drop is not a result of a decrease in foreign direct investment, which held steady in 2008, but due to a decline in bilateral portfolio investment. The banking crisis caused many lending institutions to pull their short-term investments out of developing countries and decrease their lending activities, causing an overall decline in capital flows. Thus, the drop in private flows shown in Figure 3

is largely a result of a drop in bilateral portfolio investments. Despite the volatility of capital flows, remittances and philanthropy remained stable, and when combined, greatly outnumber official flows. Figure 4 provides a breakdown of the different forms of private flows, comparing them to public flows over the last 15 years.

The OECD and the international community at large focus on official flows only when making cross-country comparisons. Figures 1 shows net ODA from each DAC donor nation, and Figure 2 shows ODA as a percentage of GNI. Most nations fail to reach the 0.7% target set by the international community. Since ODA is an incomplete measure of what a country gives to the developing world, it is more helpful to compare donors on the basis of all financial aid—ODA, philanthropy, and remittances. Figures 5, 6, and 7 provide measures of the full generosity of DAC donor countries by combining their ODA, private philanthropy, and remittance outflows to the developing world.

Measuring absolute volumes of ODA, private philanthropy, and remittances as Figure 5 does, puts the United States in

161.0

31.3

26.2

first place with $161 billion, or 45% percent of total assistance by all DAC donors. While the United States is undoubtedly the biggest contributor of total assistance, the gap between the United States and other nations will most likely get smaller in the future as research into other donors' private philanthropy continues to improve. Furthermore, the United States is likely to have more immigrants and migrant workers and thus total remittances from the United States will continue to outnumber remittances from other nations. After the United States, the next largest donors to the developing world in 2008 were the United Kingdom, Germany, France, Canada, Japan and Spain, an order which has not changed from 2007.

Figure 6 shows ODA, private philanthropy and remittance flows of the DAC countries as a percentage of GNI. If ODA is the only flow considered when measuring a nation's contributions relative to its GNI, then only five nations succeed in

121.5   52.6   180.8 354.9

reaching the target of 0.7%, as shown by Figure 2. When private philanthropy and remittances are included, however, 16 of the 22 DAC donors pass the mark. Several countries, including Canada, the United Kingdom and the United States, rank better relative to other donors once all three flows are calculated. Canada and the United States make the largest leaps when all flows are considered. Canada jumps from fifteenth to second place, mainly as a result of the large remittance outflows from Canada to developing countries, which alone make up .83% of Canada's GNI. When all flows are included, the United States jumps from last place to sixth, a result of including remittances and philanthropy in the calculation.

Figure 7 makes donor comparisons on a per capita basis. As in 2007, Luxembourg had the highest per capita assistance level at $1,111. Scandinavian countries took three of the top four spots. Norway provided the second highest per capita assistance at $1,023, Sweden the third with $698, and Denmark the fourth with $665. For the most part countries that had high levels of government assistance as measured as a percentage of GNI also had high levels of per capita assistance.

One third of the private philanthropy figures reported in these graphs are reported by donor governments to the OECD each year. These calculations are incomplete and thus inaccurate, often based on voluntary and outdated surveys

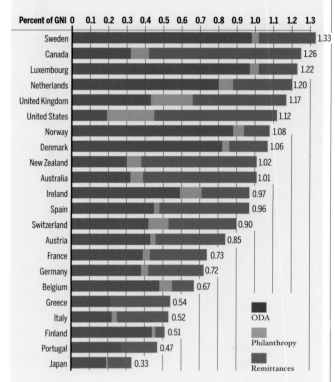

Figure 6

Total Assistance from OECD Donor Countries to Developing Countries: ODA, Philanthropy and Remittances as a Percentage of GNI, 2008

Percent of GNI	Value
Sweden	1.33
Canada	1.26
Luxembourg	1.22
Netherlands	1.20
United Kingdom	1.17
United States	1.12
Norway	1.08
Denmark	1.06
New Zealand	1.02
Australia	1.01
Ireland	0.97
Spain	0.96
Switzerland	0.90
Austria	0.85
France	0.73
Germany	0.72
Belgium	0.67
Greece	0.54
Italy	0.52
Finland	0.51
Portugal	0.47
Japan	0.33

ODA
Philanthropy
Remittances

Source: OECD, *Development Co-operation Report 2010*; Hudson Institute's remittance calculations from DAC donors to DAC recipients based on data from the World Bank's Migration and Remittance Team 2009; Stein Brothers, AB, Scandinavia 2009-2010; Charles Sellen, France, 2008-2009 and VU University Amsterdam Department of Philanthropy, Netherlands, 2009; Instituto per la Riceraca Sociale, Italy, 2009; Le Cercle de Cooperation des OND de Developpement, Annual Report, Luxenberg, 2009; Vrije Universiteit Amsterdam, Geven in Nederland 2009, Netherlands, 2009; Council on International Development, Annual Report, New Zealand, 2009; Plataforma Portuguesa das ONGD, Annual Report, Portugal, 2009; Coordinadora de ONG Para El Dessarrollo Espana, Informe de La Coordinadora de ONG Para El Desarrollo-Espana Sobre El Sector De Las ONGD, Spain, 2009; GuideStar Data Services, United Kingdom, 2009; Center for Global Prosperity, United States, 2009-2010.

of charities only. This fails to fully capture giving by corporations, foundations, and religious organizations, and excludes estimates for volunteer time. To remedy some of these deficiencies, the Hudson Institute began in 2000 to measure U.S. private giving more comprehensively. The U.S. government is aware of the inadequacies of the private giving number it reports to the OECD and has acknowledged in publications and official presentations the improved giving number developed by the research institutions in collaboration with the Hudson Institute. In the absence of a decision on using improved numbers, the government continues to submit incomplete numbers.

In an effort to better measure private giving in other donor countries, the Hudson Institute's Center for Global Prosperity (CGP) has started international partnerships with organizations across the developed world. In 2009, the CGP was able to provide larger and more accurate private giving numbers for two additional countries. This year, through our own research and that of our partners, the *Index* provides

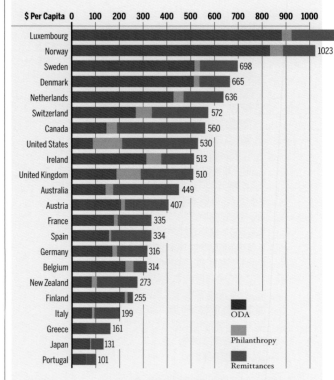

Figure 7

Total Assistance from OECD Donor Countries to Developing Countries: ODA, Philanthropy and Remittances per Capita, 2008

$ Per Capita	
Luxembourg	1111
Norway	1023
Sweden	698
Denmark	665
Netherlands	636
Switzerland	572
Canada	560
United States	530
Ireland	513
United Kingdom	510
Australia	449
Austria	407
France	335
Spain	334
Germany	316
Belgium	314
New Zealand	273
Finland	255
Italy	199
Greece	161
Japan	131
Portugal	101

Legend: ODA, Philanthropy, Remittances

Source: OECD, *Development Co-operation Report 2010*; Hudson Institute's remittance calculations from DAC donors to DAC recipients based on data from the World Bank's Migration and Remittance Team 2009; Stein Brothers, AB, Scandinavia 2009-2010; Charles Sellen, France, 2008-2009 and VU University Amsterdam Department of Philanthropy, Netherlands, 2009; Instituto per la Ricerca Sociale, Italy, 2009; Le Cercle de Cooperation des OND de Developpement, Annual Report, Luxenberg, 2009; Vrije Universiteit Amsterdam, Geven in Nederland 2009, Netherlands, 2009; Council on International Development, Annual Report, New Zealand, 2009; Plataforma Portuguesa das ONGD, Annual Report, Portugal, 2009; Coordinadora de ONG Para El Dessarrollo Espana, Informe de La Coordinadora de ONG Para El Desarrollo-Espana Sobre El Sector De Las ONGD, Spain, 2009; GuideStar Data Services, United Kingdom, 2009; Center for Global Prosperity, United States, 2009-2010.

improved data and trends for 14 of the 22 DAC donor countries: Denmark, Finland, France, Italy, Luxembourg, Norway, the Netherlands, New Zealand, Portugal, Spain, Sweden, Switzerland, the United Kingdom, and the United States.

The CGP continues to partner with GuideStar Data Services for research on private philanthropy in the United Kingdom. Peter Stein of Stein Brothers continues to be CGP's partner in obtaining giving numbers for the Scandinavian countries including Denmark, Finland, Norway, Sweden, and Switzerland. Additionally, this year CGP has for the first time partnered with Instituto per la Ricerca Sociale in Italy to obtain the Italian private giving number to the developing world. CGP is also developing a new partnership with European Research Network on Philanthropy to collaborate on future work. CGP will continue to work with these partners and form new partnerships to meet our goal of providing more accurate private giving numbers for all donor countries to the developed world. The International Philanthropy Outside of the United States chapter on page 40 discusses private giving data and trends in other donor countries at greater length.

The figures for remittances are based on World Bank data. Using the World Bank's 2006 bilateral matrix developed by William Shaw and Dilip Ratha, a compilation of weighted formulas used for estimating remittances between countries, we extrapolated to estimate remittance outflows from donor countries to the developing world in 2008. While we believe these figures are some of the best estimates available, it is important to keep in mind that all data on remittances are estimates and created using a variety of assumptions. Our discussion of remittances is in the Global Remittances chapter, beginning on page 58. Additional information on our methodology can be found in the Methodology section on page 66.

What is clear from these numbers is that developed countries provide far more to the developing world through private actors than through government aid. Figures 3, 4, 5, 6, and 7 show that private sector interactions—whether it be investment, remittances, and private philanthropy or just remittances and private philanthropy—far exceed official development assistance. This reflects the diverse, new world of international development where for-profits, nonprofits, religious organizations, universities, families and individuals can and are contributing to economic growth in the developing world.

1 Organisation for Economic Co-operation and Development, *Statistical Annex of the 2010 Development Co-Operation Report*, Table 13.

2 Dilip Ratha, "Migration and Remittances Trends 2009," Migration and Development Brief 11, World Bank, Migration and Remittances Team, November 3, 2009.

3 Caroline Preston, Nicole Wallace and Ian Wilhelm, "American Charities Raise $774 million for Haiti Relief, Chronicle Tally Finds," *The*

Chronicle of Philanthropy, February 17, 2010.

4 Ibid.

5 Agnes Teh, "Boy, 7, raises $240,000 for Haiti appeal," CNN.com, Jan. 26, 2010; Charlie's Fundraising for Haiti page, http://www.justgiving.com/CharlieSimpson-HAITI.

6 OCED, *Development Co-operation Report, 2010*.

7 Secretary of State, Hillary Rodham Clinton, The United States Emergency Plan for AIDS Relief,

Public Private Partnerships, http://www.pepfar.gov/ppp/index.htm (accessed Feb. 24, 2010).

8 Laura Rozen, "Previewing Clinton's Development Speech," *Politico*, Jan. 6, 2010.

9 Hillary Clinton, "Development in the 21st Century," Speech delivered at the Peter G. Peterson Institute for International Economics in Washington, DC, Jan. 6, 2010.

10 Andrew Sparrow, Larry Elliot, and Heather

Stewart, "Cameron unveils MyAid plan to let public vote on development priorities," *The Guardian*, July 13, 2009, http://www.guardian.co.uk/politics/2009/jul/13/cameron-myaid-development (accessed Feb. 24, 2010).

11 Steven Lawrence, "Foundations' Year-end Outlook for Giving and the Sector," Foundation Center, November 2009, http://foundationcenter.org/gainknowledge/research/pdf/researchadvisory_economy_200911.pdf (accessed February 3, 2010).

12 Ibid.

13 Ibid.

14 Steven Lawrence, "Foundations Address the Impact of the Economic Crisis," The Foundation Center Research Advisory, April 2009, http://foundationcenter.org/gainknowledge/research/pdf/researchadvisory_economy_200904.pdf,

15 Ian Wilhelm, "Ford Foundation Offers Buyouts to One-Third of Its 550 Workers," *Chronicle of Philanthropy*, June 18, 2009.

16 Mike Spector, "Ford Foundation to Close Two Overseas Offices," *The Wall Street Journal*, April 29, 2009.

17 Stephanie Strom, "New Leader Overhauls Ford Foundation," *The New York Times*, April 13, 2009, http://www.nytimes.com/2009/04/14/us/14ford.html (accessed January 21, 2010).

18 Highlights of Foundation Yearbook, The Foundation Center, http://foundationcenter.org/gainknowledge/research/pdf/fy2009_highlights.pdf (accessed February 3, 2010).

19 "The Conference Board Finds the Economic Downturn Will Have Major Effects on Corporate Philanthropy," The Conference Board, March 3, 2009, http://www.conference-board.org/utilities/pressDetail.cfm?press_id=3595 (accessed January 26, 2010).

20 Caroline Preston, "Corporate Leaders Tout Philanthropy's Benefits Amid Grim Financial News," *The Chronicle of Philanthropy*, Feb. 24, 2009.

21 Michelle Nicholas, "Bumpy Ride for Corporate Giving Amid Recession," *International Business Times*, March 5, 2010.

22 Caroline Preston, "Corporate Leaders Tout Philanthropy's Benefits Amid Grim Financial News," *The Chronicle of Philanthropy*, Feb. 24, 2009.

23 "Corporate Philanthropy Strong in 2010, Despite Economy," *The Huffington Post*, January 7, 2010 http://www.huffingtonpost.com/2010/01/07/corporate-philanthropy-st_n_415021.html (accessed February 17, 2010).

24 Phone Interview with Lori Warrens, Executive Director, Partnership for Quality Medical Donations, Jan. 26, 2010.

25 "CSR and the Financial Crisis: Taking Stock", csrinternational.blogspot.com, http://www.csrinternational.org/?tag=strategic-csr (accessed January 13, 2010).

26 A. T. Kearney, "Companies with a Commitment to Sustainability Tend to Outperform their Peers during the Financial Crisis," http://www.atkearney.com/index.php/News-media/companies-with-a-commitment-to-sustainability-tend-to-outperform-their-peers-during-the-financial-crisis.html (accessed January 21, 2010).

27 "Global Fairtrade Sales Increase by 22%," The Fairtrade Foundation, June 8, 2009, http://www.fairtrade.org.uk/press_office/press_releases_and_statements/jun_2009/global_fair trade_sales_increase_by_22.aspx (accessed January 27, 2010).

28 Rebecca Smithers, "UK spending on Fairtrade products rises despite recession," *The Guardian*, September 24, 2009, http://www.guardian.co.uk/environment/2009/sep/24/fairtrade-spending (accessed January 27, 2010).

29 Ibid.

30 Jeff Chu, "Are Fairtrade Goods Recession Proof?" *Fast Company*, March 27, 2009, http://www.fastcompany.com/blog/jeff-chu/inquisition/fair-trade-recession-proof (accessed January 27, 2010).

31 "U.S. Charitable Giving Projections 2009, 2010," February 2010, http://www.bc.edu/offices/pubaf/news/CWP_individual_giving_model2010_21.html (accessed Jan. 27, 2010).

32 Caroline Preston and Chris Thompson, "A Flurry of Last-Minute Giving Lifted Charities' Holiday Appeals," *The Chronicle of Philanthropy*, Jan 27, 2010, http://philanthropy.com/article/A-Flurry-of-Last-Minute-Giving/63490/ (accessed Jan. 27, 2010).

33 Nayna Agrawal "Asian Giving at Home and Abroad: a Practitioner's Perspective," *Advancing Philanthropy*, January/February 2010, Vol. 17, No. 1.

34 Holly Hall, "Fund Raising Goes Global to Meet Growing Needs," *The Chronicle of Philanthropy*, September 17, 2009.

35 Sarah Cassidy, "Charities forced to merge or layoff staff as economic crisis hits their funding," *The Independent*, December 8, 2009, http://www.independent.co.uk/news/uk/home-news/charities-forced-to-merge-or-lay-off-staff-as-economic-crisis-hits-their-funding-1836055.html (accessed January 28, 2010).

36 International Federation of Pharmaceutical Manufacturers Associations, http://www.ifpma.org/index.php?id=2179 (accessed January 28, 2010).

37 "Renaissance Charitable Foundation Acquires Sei Giving Fund," Renaissance press release, June 30, 2008, http://www.rcgf.org/articles-releases/RCF-SEI-merger.pdf (accessed January 28, 2010).

38 Breda Heffernan, "Aid agencies merge to streamline help for Africa," *Independent*, August 6, 2008.

39 Amy Feldman, "Rethinking How to Give," *Business Week*, Jan. 21, 2010.

40 Noelle Barton and Paula Wasley, "Size of Average Online Gift Dropped in 2008," *The Chronicle of Philanthropy*, May 14, 2009.

41 Ian Wilhelm, "Giving Around the World Faces Recession Snags," *The Chronicle of Philanthropy*, April 23, 2009.

42 Global Trends in NGO Law, International Center for Not-for-profit Law, *Quarterly Review*, Volume 1, Issue 2: Global Philanthropy in a Time of Crisis, http://www.icnl.org/knowledge/globaltrends/GloTrends1-2.htm (accessed January 28, 2010).

43 David Roodman, "History Says Financial Crisis Will Suppress Aid. Global Development: Views from the Center," http://blogs.cgdev.org/globaldevelopment/2008/10/history-says-financial-crisis.php (accessed Feb. 18, 2010).

44 Open Letter to Heads of State calling for Aid Pledge, Secretary-General Angel Gurria and Chairman Eckhard Deutscher, October 20, 2008, http://www.oecd.org/dataoecd/31/34/41613742.pdf (accessed Feb. 18, 2010).

45 "NSC Official Reaffirms Obama Pledge to Double Foreign Aid," USAID Press, August 2009, http://www.usaid.gov/press/frontlines/fl_aug09/p5_nsc080909.html (accessed January 28, 2010).

46 Organisation for Economic Co-operation and Development, *Statistical Annex of the 2010 Development Co-Operation Report*, Table 13.

47 Organisation for Economic Co-operation and Development (OECD). *2009 Development Co-Operation Report*, Paris: OECD.

48 Organisation for Economic Co-operation and Development (OECD), *OECD Journal on Development: Development Co-operation Report 2010*, Chapter 8, Paris: OECD.

49 Organisation for Economic Co-operation and Development, *Statistical Annex of the 2010 Development Co-Operation Report*, Table 01ae.

50 Organisation for Economic Co-operation and Development, *Statistical Annex of the 2010 Development Co-Operation Report*, Table 13.

51 Organisation for Economic Co-operation and Development, *Statistical Annex of the 2010 Development Co-Operation Report*, Table 01e.

52 Organisation for Economic Co-operation and Development (OECD), *OECD Journal on Development: Development Co-operation Report 2010*, Chapter 8, Paris: OECD.

53 Organisation for Economic Co-operation and Development, *Statistical Annex of the 2010 Development Co-Operation Report*, Table 01e.

54 Organisation for Economic Co-operation and Development, *Statistical Annex of the 2010 Development Co-Operation Report*, Table 25e.

55 Ibid.

56 Organisation for Economic Co-operation and Development, *Statistical Annex of the 2010 Development Co-Operation Report*, Table 01e.

57 Organisation for Economic Co-operation and Development, *Statistical Annex of the 2010 Development Co-Operation Report*, Table 01ae.

58 Organisation for Economic Co-operation and Development (OECD), *OECD Journal on Development: Development Co-operation Report 2010*, Chapter 8, Paris: OECD.

59 Ibid.

60 Bill McCormick, unpublished document, "2008 U.S. Resource Flows to Developing Countries Summary for the Final Estimates submitted to the Development Assistance Committee of the OECD," November 25, 2009.

61 Organisation for Economic Co-operation and Development, *Statistical Annex of the 2010 Development Co-Operation Report*, Table 14.

62 Bill McCormick, unpublished document, "2008 U.S. Resource Flows to Developing Countries Summary for the Final Estimates submitted to the Development Assistance Committee of the OECD," November 25, 2009.

Private Aid at Work

The Fallujah Widow's Dairy Development Project in Iraq, a partnership between the U.S. Marines, Land O'Lakes and the Women's Cultural Center in Fallujah, is working to restore the dairy industry in war-torn Fallujah.

International development assistance continues to be reinvented by U.S. philanthropic organizations. Foundations, corporations, private and voluntary organizations (PVOs), individual volunteers, colleges and universities, and religious organizations are reinventing how funding for international development assistance is collected and distributed. They are at the forefront of efforts to require more transparency, accountability and sustainability in international development projects. The following pages measure the giving by these key segments of private donors in the United States. They also contain success stories that illustrate innovative philanthropic projects around the world.

FUNDING INNOVATION

Foundations: $4.3 Billion

Independent, community, and grant-making operating foundations in the United States gave a total of $4.3 billion to developing countries in 2008, according to Foundation Center research conducted for the Center for Global Prosperity. This represents a $700 million increase over the revised 2007 total of $3.6 billion.

Health and medical services account for 52% of all international grant dollars from U.S. foundations, followed by democracy and governance at 23% and economic growth and trade (including environmental grants) at 16%. Education accounted for 4% of grant funds and disaster relief and refugees accounted for 1%, and all other areas were 4%.

A total of 71% of all international grants awarded in 2008 by U.S. foundations were multi-regional grants or grants for unspecified countries. Of the remaining 29%, the single largest recipient of U.S. foundation money was Asia and the Pacific at 12.8%, followed by sub-Saharan Africa at 9.9%, followed by Latin America and the Caribbean at 4.5%, Europe and Central Asia at 1.6%, and North Africa and the Middle East at less than one percent.

International grantmaking by U.S. foundations reached a record high in 2008 after increasing at a record pace between 2002 and 2008. International grantmaking is expected to be affected by the recession along with other sectors of foundation giving in 2009. Overall, the Foundation Center predicts a 10% decline in U.S. foundation giving in 2009 and forecasts declining or flat giving through 2010.[1]

The prospects for international giving may be less dire than for other sectors. According to a 2008 survey of international grantmakers by the Council on Foundations and the Foundation Center, over half of the survey respondents said they expected international funding by U.S. foundations to grow

over the next two to three years and just over one-quarter said they expected it to remain the same.[2] Major international grantmakers interviewed for the survey said they are committed to overseas giving and that international funding remains a long-term commitment for funders and an integral part of their overall giving strategies.[3]

Efforts are underway throughout the foundation community to ensure that resources are utilized efficiently. The John D. and Catherine T. MacArthur Foundation uses the MacArthur Award for Creative and Effective Institutions to reward emerging organizations that demonstrate creativity, drive, and vision and are paving the way for more effective ways of delivering services or providing new ways to look at problems related to poverty and development.

MacArthur Foundation
Sparking Innovation

Few foundations match the worldwide scope and ambition of the John D. and Catherine T. MacArthur Foundation. From global issues such as human rights and sustainable development to domestic concerns in the United States, the foundation has a history of supporting organizations that demonstrate creativity, drive, and vision. Each year, the foundation selects a small group of U.S. and overseas nonprofit organizations that embody these qualities for recognition with the MacArthur Award for Creative and Effective Institutions.

The award recognizes small or emerging organizations that generate provocative ideas, are particularly effective at delivering services, or provide new ways of looking at existing problems. The award is given to organizations with budgets of less than $5 million annually that previously have received support from the MacArthur Foundation. The organization must have reached a critical point in its development and demonstrate exceptional creativity and effectiveness as well as strong leadership and stable financial management. Winning organizations receive between $350,000 and $650,000, depending on the size of their operating budget.

Winners of the award include the Caribbean Natural Resources Institute in Trinidad (2009), which has built alliances among the region's governments and organizations to resolve conflicts between environmental and development goals, and the Legal Defense and Assistance Project in Nigeria (2008), which is working to reform Nigeria's criminal defense system.

One of the 2006 winners, the Society for Education, Action, and Research in Community Health (SEARCH), demonstrates the blend of cutting edge service delivery and organizational excellence that characterizes the award winners. SEARCH was founded in 1985 by Dr. Abhay Bang and his wife Dr. Rani Bang to address the high rate of maternal and infant mortality in rural India. The Bangs were eager to combine their master's degrees in public health from Johns Hopkins University with a direct, community-based approach to healthcare delivery. "Always begin with what people need and then build upon their strengths and potential to enable them to do what they need," advised Dr. Bang.

SEARCH combines innovative, community-based healthcare delivery methods with rigorous research trials of these interventions to influence local and international healthcare delivery. One of SEARCH's landmark programs was based on a five-year field trial in the Gadchiroli district that found that neonatal mortality could be reduced 62% by training village women to become community health workers. These "barefoot neonatologists," as Dr. Bang calls them, have been trained to diagnose and treat common illnesses in newborns. The program, which is now operating in 40 villages, has resulted in a 70% decline in newborn deaths. This pioneering approach to neonatal care is being implemented throughout India and in other developing countries such as Nepal and Bangladesh.

Dr. Abhay Bang, co-founder of SEARCH, which received the MacArthur Award for Creative and Effective Institutions for its innovative, community-based healthcare programs in rural India.

The incidence of child labor in the handwoven rug industry in India, Nepal and Pakistan has decreased to an estimated 250,000 from 1 million when RugMark started in 1995. RugMark has freed more than 3,600 children from the looms.

Today, SEARCH provides community healthcare to 100,000 in the Gadchiroli district, with a specific focus on women, children and tribal peoples. It has trained 200 part-time workers selected from the community to help with SEARCH's mission. In addition, the organization provides hospital-level healthcare, alcohol prevention and de-addiction, and reproductive health education to one million people in three districts. It conducts rigorous studies to evaluate the impact of its work and uses the information to revamp or redirect its efforts. Dr. Bang and his wife have received numerous awards for their contributions to healthcare and were named "Global Health Heroes" by *Time* magazine.

The MacArthur Foundation believes that the knowledge SEARCH gains from its continued investigation and analysis will help governments in India and around the world develop better tools for informed, effective public health solutions.

–Emily P. Gikow

HUMANITY UNITED
The Seal of Approval

Slavery is a term that most people associate with the past. But in his groundbreaking 2003 *National Geographic* article, "21st Century Slaves," Andrew Cockburn estimated that there are some 27 million enslaved people around the world today. According to Free the Slaves, this includes bonded laborers forced to work for free to pay off their families' debt, women and girls who are kidnapped and forced to work in brothels, and children who are sold by desperately poor families. What they all have in common is being forced to work for free under the threat of violence and being unable to leave their "employer."

Pam Omidyar became concerned about the lack of donor awareness of anti-slavery issues after she read Cockburn's article. She started Humanity United in 2005 as a grantmaking organization focused on ending slavery. "Over the past few years, we have come to understand that an effective, long-term strategy to ending these injustices must involve fundamental changes in the laws and norms that allow these practices to continue," she said.

The Silicon Valley-based organization is one of largest donors in the anti-slavery movement, providing between $16 to $25 million annually to about 100 grantees. One of its major grantees is RugMark, a grant recipient since 2007. RugMark is an international PVO working to end widespread child labor in the profitable handmade rug industry in South Asia, where the use of child labor is the norm. Nina Smith, the executive director of RugMark in America, said children are used "because they are cheap, easily controlled and less likely to object to their treatment or conditions of work."

According to Smith, many factory owners claim that child workers are "apprentices," but the truth is that close to 90% of children in the industry are not paid and have been sold by their families for a small sum. Under RugMark's GoodWeave program, rug producers and importers agree to adhere to strict no-child-labor guidelines and be subject to random factory inspections. In return for this pledge, they receive the right to display the GoodWeave seal on their rugs. More than 5.5 million carpets bearing the GoodWeave label have been sold in Europe and North America. "Our aim is to build a market preference for child-labor free rugs throughout the supply chain," said Smith.

When RugMark inspectors find a child working at a rug loom, they offer the child the opportunity to go to school, either at home with RugMark support or at a RugMark-funded boarding school. Income generated by the licensing of the GoodWeave seal is used by RugMark to fund educational, rehabilitation, literacy, and vocational training programs in India and Nepal.

The incidence of child labor in the handwoven rug industry in India, Nepal and Pakistan has decreased to an estimated 250,000 from 1 million when RugMark started in 1995. "It's really a combination of direct rescue efforts, deterrence and indirect effort from generating greater awareness along the supply chain and stakeholders," says Smith.

RugMark has directly freed more than 3,600 children from the looms. One of these children is Sunita Jimba, who is from a tiny village in the Sarlahi District of Nepal. Jimba was sold to a broker for the equivalent of $2.50 by her desperately poor family. She was forced to weave rugs from four in the morning until late at night and endure beatings from the factory owner. Jimba was scared when a RugMark inspector discovered her and brought her to one of the organization's rehabilitation centers, but she quickly came to enjoy living at the center and going to school. Today, Jimba dreams of becoming a teacher and is happy just to be free.   —Ai Gee Ong

The Skoll Foundation
A Lot of Good from a Little Bit of Good

As the first president of the pioneering Internet auction site eBay, Jeff Skoll had a front-row seat to the power of entrepreneurship. When he retired from eBay, he decided to use his personal fortune to encourage social entrepreneurship. He founded the Skoll Foundation in 1999 to make strategic investments in innovative projects that he believes will drive large-scale social change. Skoll supports projects in which a "lot of good comes from a little bit of good"—those in which the social returns greatly outweigh the money and effort invested.

Today the Silicon Valley-based Skoll Foundation has total assets of $985 million and is active in three areas promoting social entrepreneurship. First, the foundation connects entrepreneurs through Social Edge, an online community for social entrepreneurs that reaches over 60,000 entrepreneurs a month. Second, it celebrates entrepreneurs during its annual Skoll World Forum on Social Entrepreneurship in Oxford and through broadcast partnerships with the Sundance Institute, PBS, and NPR. Third, the annual Skoll Awards for Social Entrepreneurship (SASE) support social entrepreneurs whose work has the potential for large-scale impact on the issues of tolerance and human rights; health; economic and social equity; peace and security; institutional responsibility; and environmental sustainability.

The awards provide unrestricted, three-year grants to social entrepreneurs who have tested and proved their approach and are ready to replicate or scale up. Since its inception in 2005, 60 social entrepreneurs have been awarded grants. The projects span the globe and today's most pressing social needs, from an effort to restore health and education programs in Afghanistan, to an innovative microcredit program in Paraguay, to a grassroots program in Africa that trains and employs new mothers with HIV to provide education and support to their peers. In 2009, The Skoll Foundation awarded some $30 million to nine new SASE recipients and renewed funding for several previous grantees.

The grants provide core support to help organizations expand their programs and capacity to deliver long-term change. The SASE program is unique in that it funds models and ideas, not causes or geographic regions, and only invests in programs that have had a history of measured impact. Bruce Lowry, Communications Director for the Skoll Foundation, notes that "social entrepreneurial models have solutions that are inherently effective," adding that "SASE seeks to identify social entrepreneurs that are having huge impact potential and to push them forward and help them out."

KickStart, a 2005 SASE award recipient, featured in the first *Index of Global Philanthropy* in 2006, illustrates the power of the entrepreneurial model. Nick Moon and Martin Fisher founded KickStart in 1991 to develop and promote technologies that could be used to establish and run profitable small-scale enterprises in Kenya. In 1998, they developed an inexpensive, manually operated pump that can draw water uphill from shallow water sources—a key need for many farmers in Africa—and irrigate up to two acres of land. This simple but powerful technology has allowed farmers to grow crops year round, plant a greater diversity of crops, and improve their yields, improving both their diets and their ability to sell high-value crops. Since its inception, the organization has helped 77,000 families in Africa create profitable businesses, generating $85 million per year in new profits and wages.

Thanks to support from the Skoll award, KickStart has been able to expand its business in eastern Africa. "Working with Skoll has really been tremendous and has way more than doubled our impact" says Ken Weimar, senior director for Development with KickStart. "In 2002 KickStart was selling 7,000 pumps a year. As of fiscal year 2009, KickStart is selling 27,000 pumps a year."

Skoll's ability to leverage its resources to multiply its impact around the world caused Barron's to recently name the relatively small foundation as the number two "best giver" in the world, a designation that Jeffrey Skoll surely won't argue with.

                                                                —Andrew Baltes

Dikembe Mutombo: An Athlete With a Heart

At seven-foot-two, sporting size 22 basketball shoes (the largest in the NBA) and ranking first in rebounds per game, Dikembe Mutombo stands out in many ways. However, it's not just his size or talent that sets this basketball star apart but his ongoing commitment to the people of his homeland, the Democratic Republic of Congo.

The 44-year-old recently retired Houston Rockets' center came to Georgetown University in 1987 on an academic scholarship. He planned to become a doctor and return home to practice medicine. But an invitation by the Georgetown basketball coach John Thompson to try out for the team during his sophomore year changed everything. After a successful college basketball career, he was drafted by the Denver Nuggets. Mutombo played for the Nuggets, the Atlanta Hawks, and, eventually, the Houston Rockets, racking up honors that included being an eight-time NBA Allstar and a four-time Defensive Player of the Year.

But Mutombo's true passion has been improving the health and quality of life of the people of the Democratic Republic of Congo. He founded the Dikembe Mutombo Foundation in 1997 to focus on primary health care and disease prevention, health research, and increased access to health care education for the people of his homeland. "My inspiration in life has always been changing the living conditions of my people—anywhere in Africa," Mutombo said. "That is something I want to see happen not tomorrow, but now."

NBA Allstar Dikembe Mutombo shined on the basketball court and now shines off court, dedicating himself to improving healthcare for the people of the Democratic Republic of Congo.

The foundation has shipped medical supplies to Kinshasa, the Congo's capital, led immunization campaigns affecting millions of children, purchased ambulances for hospitals, donated computers to colleges, provided scholarships for higher education, and on the largest scale, built a hospital in Kinshasa. The Biamba Marie Mutombo Hospital and Research Center was named after Mutombo's mother, who died because of a lack of hospital facilities in Kinshasa. The hospital, which was built in conjunction with Medical Missions for Children, has 300 beds, three operating rooms, an outpatient clinic, emergency room, and pharmacy. Since opening in December 2007, the hospital has treated 25,000 patients and sees more than 150 patients everyday in the emergency room, many at no cost. The hospital also serves as a training facility for doctors.

Mutombo is the largest contributor to the foundation and donated $19 million of his own money to build the hospital. The foundation also receives donations from individuals and has partnerships with Qualcomm, Lenovo,

the NBA, and the University of North Carolina. Qualcomm provides high speed wireless service and devices for the hospital, which allows it to link to its "sister" hospital in Escondido, CA. Lenovo provides IT infrastructure, computers and consulting services for the hospital and funds the Lenovo Fellowship, which enables residents from the University of North Carolina Hospital to work alongside physicians in the Mutombo Hospital.

In addition to his work with his foundation, Mutombo has traveled around Africa giving free basketball clinics for upwards of 2,000 children a day and was the first Youth Emissary for the United Nations Development Programme. In 2007, he joined the Board of Advisors for the microfinance organization Opportunity International. In 2000, President Bill Clinton awarded Mutombo the President's Service Award, and in 2007, he was inducted into the World Sports Humanitarian Hall of Fame. He won the "Most Caring Athlete Award" from USA Weekend, and was named by FOXSports.com as the most generous athlete in the world.

Touring the Biamba Marie Mutombo Hospital in August of 2009 with U.S. Secretary of State Hillary Clinton, Mutombo said, "This hospital was such a dream and today is a reality and serving the community of more than 3 million people. We think that Congolese people deserve better health care, and we hope that what we are doing here, we're just setting an example so that people can have hope." —Zenah Hasan

Corporations: $7.7 Billion

U.S. corporations contributed $7.7 billion to international development assistance causes in 2008. This is a $900 million increase over the 2007 figure of $6.8 billion and reflects the corporate community's increased attention to the developing world. The Center for Global Philanthropy worked with the Committee Encouraging Corporate Philanthropy (CECP), The Foundation Center, the Urban Institute, and the Partnership for Quality Medical Donations to calculate corporate giving to the developing world.

The CECP included questions on corporate giving to the developing world specifically for the *Index* in its 2008 Corporate Philanthropy Survey. U.S. companies responding to the survey reported $167 million in international giving in 2008. The Foundation Center through its survey of corporate foundations found that $272 million of corporate foundation giving went to the developing world in 2008. Based on PVO's tax filings for 2008 as measured by the Urban Institute's Center on Nonprofits and Philanthropy for in-kind drugs and medical supplies and transport and other handling costs incurred mostly by corporations donating these in-kind contributions, we calculate total pharmaceutical and medical donations to the developing world at $7 billion. Finally, CGP staff conducted an extensive review of 350 Fortune 500 companies not reporting through CECP. We reviewed annual reports, conducted Internet searches, and contacted companies by phone, tallying a total of $274 million in cash and in-kind giving.

International giving continues to be a growing priority for U.S. corporations. According to CECP's *Giving in Numbers* report, U.S. companies directed 13% of their giving internationally in 2008, up from 12% in 2007. Certain segments of the U.S. corporate community are even more generous. Fortune 100 companies on average directed 18% of total giving to international recipients in 2008, and companies that generated 30% or more of their revenue abroad directed 23% of their contributions internationally. The health care industry was the largest single corporate giving sector in 2008, directing 27% of its giving abroad.[4]

Despite the recession, corporate philanthropy leaders said they expect funding to increase for international causes because of its strategic importance to many companies.[5] Stanley Litow, president of the IBM International Foundation, said: "If it's about spare change, and pure generosity, then it's going to be subject to economic changes, up or down. If it's tied to your business strategy and is building shareholder value, then it will fare well because it will be about real change."[6]

International corporate volunteering (ICV) also continues to increase. In 2008, 49% of CECP surveyed companies had at least one ICV program, up from 42% in 2007.[7] More than 150 participants from corporations and PVOs gathered in Beijing in December 2009 for the 2009 Corporate Volunteer International Forum to hear about cutting-edge ICV programs, including CISCO's volunteer matching donation system and Microsoft's 3 Paid Volunteer Days program, in which international employees are provided three days of paid time to volunteer in their local communities.[8]

> International giving continues to be a priority for U.S. corporations. U.S. companies directed 13% of their giving internationally in 2008, up from 12% in 2007. Fortune 100 companies directed 18% of total giving to international recipients.

WHOLE PLANET FOUNDATION
Seeds of Prosperity

John Mackey knows as well as anyone you have to start somewhere. He was only 25 in 1978 when he started his first business with a loan from his father, co-founding one of the first natural foods stores. Today, Whole Foods Market is one of the most recognizable names in the natural foods business, with sales topping $5.7 billion and a spot on the Fortune 500 List.

A firm believer in free market principles, Mackey established the Whole Planet Foundation in October 2005 to enable poor entrepreneurs in the developing world to access microcredit loans. In 2006, the Whole Planet Foundation provided its first loan to Grameen Bank for a microfinance program in Costa Rica. Since then, the foundation's loan program has grown dramatically, nearing $13 million in 2009. Today it serves more than 40,000 recipients in 15 countries that supply products to Whole Foods stores, giving priority to projects that demonstrate financial leverage and sustainability.

Recently, the Whole Planet Foundation partnered with Mercy Corps, a world-renowned PVO, and the Nirdhan Utthan Bank, a Nepali-owned microfinance institution, to assist poor farmers in the Mechi province of Nepal, which supplies Whole Foods with tea. Whole Planet Foundation has committed $312,000 over the next three years to Mercy Corps and Nirdhan Utthan Bank to expand access to finance and distribute $3.5 million worth of loans to 10,000 poor farmers to help them escape the cycle of poverty.

Loans have been provided to 1,344 farmers, including Dilkumari Gole Tamang, a 26-year-old Nepali woman who runs her family's small farm while her husband works as a security guard in Malaysia. She recently joined the Women's Microfinance Group in her village and received a loan of 20,000 Nepalese rupees (about $260) from the Nirdhan Utthan Bank, which she used to buy ginger seeds and two goats. With her newly acquired resources, she hopes to get a four-fold return from her farm this year. She plans on using the profits to expand her farming business and to buy a cow so she can sell milk. In the long term, she hopes her increased profits will allow her to provide an education for her six-year-old son.

Working with poor farmers in remote areas has many challenges, according to Jarrod Fath, manager of communications for Mercy Corps in Nepal. He noted that the flexibility of the Whole Planet Foundation has been important in facilitating innovation in rural agricultural finance. Traditional models of microfinance require regular meetings and monthly repayments that do not suit the situations of cardamom and ginger farmers in Nepal, who earn most of their cash at harvest time. Working with Whole Planet, a microfinance model has been developed that permits a high degree of flexibility. "Whole Planet has supported us and been flexible. It has worked out quite well," said Jarrod.

Whole Planet Foundation is proud of its role in changing the lives of people like Dilkumari Tamang and sees her newfound ability to increase her modest income as one small step in unleashing the energy and creativity of every person to create wealth and prosperity.

—**Jason M. Farrell**

Through grants to partners in Nepal, Whole Planet Foundation has improved the lives of many poor farmers, including this ginger farmer in Mechi.

MERCK & CO., INC.

Accessing Hope

The mountain kingdom of Lesotho in southern Africa has the third highest cervical cancer rate in the world, after Haiti and Tanzania. At 61.6 cases per 100,000 women, it is almost twice that of southern Africa and four times the global rate. The principal cause of cervical cancer is infection by the sexually transmitted human papillomavirus (HPV). Approximately 80% of cervical cancer cases occur in developing countries, where it is the leading cause of cancer-related deaths among women. Today there are two protective HPV vaccines for girls and young women, making cervical cancer one of the most preventable types of cancer.

In 2007, Merck & Co., Inc., pledged to make available at least three million doses of GARDASIL, its quadrivalent HPV vaccine, free of charge to qualifying organizations and institutions in developing countries. According to Kris Natarajan, Director of Global Health Partnerships at Merck, a vital aspect of the

Girls in Lesotho wait in line to receive the GARDASIL HPV vaccine. Under Merck's GARDASIL Access Program, 40,000 girls in Lesotho will receive the vaccine.

GARDASIL Access Program is that "by sharing operational experiences and lessons learned, participants are contributing to the body of public knowledge regarding HPV vaccination and successful strategies for adolescent immunization in developing countries."

The GARDASIL Access Program is managed by Axios Healthcare Development, a U.S.-based nonprofit, with guidance from an independent advisory board composed of international public health experts. Axios approves applications based on Advisory Board recommendations and coordinates vaccine delivery.

As of February 2010, the GARDASIL Access Program had approved applications from 18 organizations and institutions in 17 developing countries, with a combined coverage of more than 165,000 girls. The program has already shipped 40% of the approved doses of GARDASIL to seven partners. Program participants span the public, private and nonprofit sectors in countries including Bhutan, Bolivia, Haiti, Uzbekistan and Lesotho. Partnerships are a crucial element of the program and approval by each country's Ministry of Health is an essential condition for participation.

In Lesotho, the Ministry of Health and Social Welfare partnered with the Lesotho-Boston Health Alliance (LeBoHA), a program run by Boston University Medical School. Through the GARDASIL Access Program, this partnership received 126,400 doses of GARDASIL to vaccinate approximately 40,000 girls in two districts (HPV vaccine is administered in a three-dose series).

As with any immunization program, there have been many lessons learned. Because GARDASIL requires three injections over a six-month period, the partners faced challenges

reaching girls for the full course. Torrential rainfall delayed transportation to remote areas, which disrupted the immunization schedule in schools, the primary points of vaccination. The impacted girls were therefore encouraged to visit nearby health centers, where trained health workers administered the vaccine. The partners also used Lesotho Defense Force helicopters to deliver vaccine teams and supplies to the remote mountain locations, home to more than 1,000 eligible girls. Specially trained health care providers evaluated all potential recipients prior to immunization to ensure they had no contraindications to the vaccine.

Because public understanding of cervical cancer and the role of HPV vaccination was virtually nonexistent in Lesotho, the partnership employed a comprehensive public information campaign. The Minister of Health and Social Welfare spearheaded a community education initiative via television, radio, posters and leaflets. Radio programs proved especially important in addressing concerns and misinformation regarding the HPV vaccine. One-on-one outreach to community and religious leaders was also critical to the success of the program. Staff from LeBoHA and the Ministry of Health and Social Welfare visited every village to meet community leaders and host public question-and-answer sessions, which successfully informed and educated communities about HPV vaccination, according to LeBoHA country representative Senate Matete.

By October 2009, more than 32,000 adolescent girls in Lesotho had received all three doses of GARDASIL. The vaccination project continues to progress in both districts and is on track to reach 40,000 girls. Through the GARDASIL Access Program, the partnership's experiences and lessons learned will contribute to the public knowledge base on HPV vaccination and adolescent immunization models in developing countries.

—Haein Lim

LAND O' LAKES

Dairy Diplomacy

U.S. Marines are employing an inventive tactic in the war-torn city of Fallujah in Iraq's Anbar province: dairy diplomacy. War has ravaged the area's once-thriving dairy industry. Today, only 10% of the region's dairy needs are met by local production. In addition, many widows

> The hope is that not only will the dairy business provide a livelihood for formerly marginalized women, but the income will allow them to send their children to school, making them more likely to be productive members of society.

in the region are poor and underemployed, leaving them mired in poverty. The U.S. Marines, in partnership with the Women's Cultural Center in Fallujah and Land O' Lakes International Development Division, sensed the potential to revitalize the dairy sector in Anbar province and provide sustainable employment to the women of Fallujah.

The Fallujah Widow's Dairy Development Program opened for business in the fall of 2008 when the Marines purchased 50 local cows, 44 of which were pregnant, and distributed them to 50 widows in the Fallujah region. The women sell milk from the cows to a mobile milk collection facility, which provides them with a stable income. In phase two of the program, launched in early 2009, Land O' Lakes International Development Division, a subsidiary of the U.S.-based dairy cooperative, provided training and technical assistance to the women in animal husbandry and milk production. Hands-on training from Land O' Lakes dairy experts enabled the women to improve the quality and quantity of the milk, increasing their incomes. In recent decades, the Land O' Lakes International Development Division has leveraged their expertise in the dairy business to support more than 160 development projects in 75 countries that generate economic growth, improve health and nutrition, and alleviate poverty.

In phase three of the project, in January 2010, the Marines and Land O' Lakes built a centralized milk collection plant to provide local employment opportunities and to allow dairy farmers to pasteurize, package, and distribute milk directly to the local market. According to Zaheer Baber, regional director for Asia and the Middle East for Land O'Lakes' International Development Division, the dairy plant will have the capacity to collect and process 1,000 liters of milk a day and will supply milk and yogurt to local restaurants and other institutions.

The Marines and Land O' Lakes are supporting the plant during the initial stages of operation, but plan to hand its management over to the local women. "One of the goals of this pilot program is to do one of these projects very well, learn, and make it successful for all, including project partners and the owners of the plant," said Baber.

The hope is that not only will the dairy business provide a livelihood for formerly marginalized women, but the income also will allow them to send their children to school, making them more likely to become productive members of society and less likely to be recruited by terrorist organizations. The partners hope to replicate the model in additional regions in Iraq and have received inquiries from individuals and government officials in other cities who want to undertake similar projects.

—Andrew Baltes

GRASSROOTS ACTION

PVOs: $11.8 Billion

Private and voluntary organizations (PVOs) contributed $11.8 billion in private funding to the developing world in 2008, a $1 billion increase over the 2007 total of $10.8 billion. The CGP once again collaborated with the Urban Institute's Center on Nonprofits and Philanthropy to determine the dollar value of international private support from private and voluntary organizations.

Of the total amount contributed by PVOs for international relief and development causes, 38% went to disaster relief and refugees, 26% went to economic growth and trade, 23% went to health and medical services, 11% went to education, and 2% went to democracy and governance. Regionally, 40% went to Latin America and the Caribbean, 25% went to sub-Saharan Africa, 19% went to Asia (excluding Central Asia), 12% went to Europe and Central Asia, and 4% went to the Middle East and North Africa.

United States-based PVOs are consolidating operations and cutting back on staff to maintain programs in the face of the global recession. World Neighbors, a 60-year-old Oklahoma-based nonprofit organization that focuses on building the knowledge base and skills necessary for development in 15 poor countries, saw its budget drop from $10 million to $6 million. The organization has undertaken a "substantial organizational restructuring" in response.[9] As with other sectors of the philanthropy community, the downturn is forcing organizations to be more creative and cooperative. To counter a drop in giving, the U.S. Committee for the United Nations Development Program, a U.S.-based nonprofit that raises money for the United Nations Development Program, has turned to the Internet and social networking sites. It now has two Facebook sites with more than 2,000 members, a blog, a Twitter account and a page on Care2, a social networking site for activists.[10]

In May 2009, InterAction, an alliance of 180 U.S.-based international PVOs, hosted a forum for members to discuss approaches to the economic crisis. According to Barbara Wallace, InterAction vice-president for membership, "innovative solutions for tight resources" included sharing projects and staff, collaborating in new ways, and mergers and acquisitions to "keep the projects going but inside a different structure."[11] Other PVOs have sharpened their focus in response to the recession. Catholic Relief Services accelerated a plan to reduce services in East Asia, Eastern Europe and South America in favor of expanded programs in Africa, South Asia and the Middle East from three years to six months in response to a decreased budget. CRS also cut some of its overseas staff and reduced benefits for U.S.-based staff. Similarly, CARE has reduced benefits and cut staff salaries to avoid cutting programs. It also financed a documentary called "A Powerful Noise" about three women making a difference in developing countries thanks to CARE. The film debuted nationally at 450 theaters in conjunction with a live streamed panel discussion with former Secretary of State Madeleine Albright and actress Natalie Portman to bring CARE's work to the attention of a new generation of potential funders.[12]

Volunteer Time: $3.6 Billion

Based on an analysis of data from the U.S. Current Population Survey's (CPS) annual volunteering supplement and Independent Sector's annual calculation of the dollar value of volunteer time, the Center for Global Prosperity determined that Americans contributed an estimated $3.6 billion worth of volunteer time in 2008 for relief and development assistance causes abroad and for international assistance organizations in the United States. The estimate for 2008

> To counter a drop in giving, the U.S. Committee for the United Nations Development Program has turned to the Internet and social networking sites. It now has two Facebook sites, a blog, and a Twitter account.

volunteer time is higher than the 2007 figure for two reasons. While the number of volunteers who traveled abroad slightly decreased, the number of individuals who volunteered for an international organization in the United States increased by 35%. Second, the value of an hour of volunteer time increased from $19.51 in 2007 to $20.25 in 2008.

While the impact of the recession on overseas volunteering is still unclear, there has been a surge in older Americans looking to volunteer abroad. The Peace Corps reports that applications from adults over the age of 50 were up 44% in 2008.[13] Organizations that arrange voluntourism trips also report more older volunteers who have either lost their job or taken early retirement. New York-based Cross-Cultural Solutions reported a 10% increase in volunteers over the age of 50 in 2008, while California-based Global Services Corps saw a 25% increase. Austin-based Alliance Abroad Group has created two new programs in Costa Rica and Ecuador specifically for older adults due to surging demand.[14]

With the popularity of international volunteering expected to continue to increase in the long-run, popular travel web sites like Travelocity.com are partnering with voluntourism organizations to make it easy for short-term international volunteers to find the perfect project. Travelocity's "Travel for Good" program partners with Global Aware, the EarthWatch Institute, Cross-Cultural Solutions and the American Hiking Society to offer voluntourism projects around the world, from conserving Amazonian dolphins to caring for people with disabilities in the rural Himalayan town of Dharamsala.[15] Travelocity also offers Change Ambassador Grants that fund voluntourism trips up to $5,000 for individuals with a demonstrated history of volunteer commitment who can't otherwise afford the travel and lodging costs of a voluntourism trip.[16]

CURE INTERNATIONAL
Putting Their Best Foot Forward

Jevason was born with clubfoot, a common, correctable congenital deformity that makes it difficult or impossible to walk. Clubfoot, which occurs in 220,000 newborn children around the world each year, can be easily corrected in young children using the Ponseti method, a simple procedure involving a series of casts over six to eight weeks, at a cost of only $250. But because Jevason was born to a poor family in Kenya, he had no access to the procedure and faced the prospect of life as a dependent, unable to get work and shunned by those around him.

But thanks to CURE International, Jevason doesn't face this grim future. His mother was directed to a clinic run by CURE International, where his clubfoot was successfully cured. Jevason is now taking steps toward a normal life.

Jevason's story is just one of thousands made possible by CURE International, which treats children with disabilities throughout the developing world. The idea for CURE was born in 1986 when Scott and Sally Harrison visited Malawi and saw how a disability could destroy a child's life. "What made the situation even more excruciating to me as an orthopedic surgeon was that I saw that these conditions could be treated and cured" said Dr. Harrison.

CURE was established in 1996. Since that time, it has seen some one million patients and performed more than 70,000 surgeries, making it the largest provider of pediatric specialty surgical care in the developing world. CURE operates 10 hospitals in Afghanistan, the Dominican Republic, Ethiopia, Honduras, Kenya, Malawi, Uganda, the United Arab Emirates and Zambia and is building a hospital in Niger.

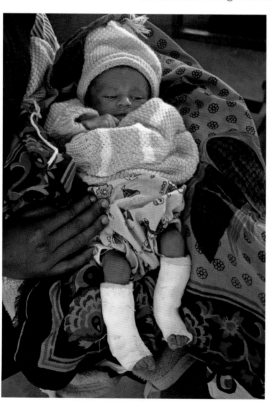

Thanks to Cure International, more than 8,000 children in developing countries have been cured of clubfoot using a simple procedure involving a series of casts.

CURE's campaign to eliminate clubfoot in the developing world, CURE Clubfoot Worldwide, was launched in 2006 and is operating in 14 countries. It has treated and cured clubfoot in more than 8,000 children. According to Executive Director Andrew Mayo, about 700 children in Kenya were cured in 2009, which means that half of all children born with clubfoot in Kenya in 2009 received treatment from CURE. In Malawi, CURE reached 80% of children born with clubfoot, and in Zambia they reached 70%. "This is a huge breakthrough," says Mayo. "It clearly demonstrates that a well organized countrywide program, run entirely from within the country, can reach a significant portion of the entire population in a relatively short period of time."

To make the program sustainable, CURE trains local medical professionals to perform the procedures. "One-hundred percent of all the surgeons that participate in the clubfoot program are local nationals," says Mayo. Ideally, he says, there will come a time when CURE is no longer involved in the program, as there are enough local surgeons trained to provide the procedure and government health ministries will pay for it.

Mayo says that what distinguishes CURE from many other nonprofits providing healthcare in the developing world is its business-like approach. "Some organizations rely on missionary surgeons, who have to go back to their homes and raise support. Our surgeons are on a salary, fundraising is totally separate," he says. In addition, CURE facilities receive income by treating adults. "Our hospital in the United Arab Emirates is totally self sustaining thanks to its private patient care, and our hospital in Malawi generates a significant portion of its revenue in-country," he notes.

Most of CURE's support, however, comes from individuals in the United States, who provide about 90% of the organization's funding. In 2007, CURE received $24 million in donations and just over $1.5 million in government support; only about 10% of CURE's budget goes to fundraising and administration. As a result, CURE receives a four-star rating from Charity Navigator, the highest rating given to nonprofit organizations that show exceptional financial management for six consecutive years.

If CURE Clubfoot Worldwide continues its current success, clubfoot may soon be a distant memory in much of the developing world.

—**Eimear O'Leary-Barrett**

LIGHT YEARS IP

More than a Cup of Coffee

Ethiopian Harrar coffee, a gourmet blend sought by coffee connoisseurs the world over, is sold for as much as $20 a pound. But until recently, Ethiopian coffee farmers only received about $1 for the same pound of coffee. Harrar, and other fine Ethiopian coffees renowned for their richness, were a potential premium commodities boon for Ethiopia, where approximately 15 million people are involved in coffee production, but local farmers were not profiting from their distinctive coffee heritage.

Light Years IP, a nonprofit organization specializing in intellectual property strategy, is dedicated to remedying situations like this around the world. Founded in 2001 by intellectual property consultant Ron Layton, Light Years works with indigenous producers in developing countries to identify and capture ownership of their intellectual property as a solution to long-term poverty alleviation. Light Years is funded by grants from organizations such as the Shell Foundation, the World Bank, and the UK Department Fund for International Development. The Washington, DC-based nonprofit works with clients in Latin America, Asia, and Africa.

Layton, who began his career working in development for the New Zealand government, realized that most developing countries could not be competitive in manufacturing due to their remote locations and the oversupply of manufacturing capacity around the world. He realized that intangible value— the ownership of a brand or manufacturing license or a creative product— is now the central means to create income in most industries, constituting up to 95% of the price of a product.

The Ethiopian Coffee Trademarking and Licensing Initia-

Intangible value is now the central means to create income in most industries. In addition to the coffee sector in Ethiopia, Light Years IP has worked with producers of Darjeeling Tea in India, chocolate in Ghana and tequila in Mexico.

tive illustrates Light Year's success. At the start of the project, growers of Ethiopian fine coffees were capturing less than 10% of the coffee's retail price, which barely covered the cost of production. In comparison, growers of Jamaica's well known Blue Mountain brand coffee were capturing 45% of its retail price. Light Years worked with stakeholders in the Ethiopian coffee sector, including coffee farmers, cooperatives, exporters, and distributors, to create a long-term strategy for brand management and promotion. This included securing trademarks for the names of fine Ethiopian coffees, to build brand recognition around the world.

As a result, Ethiopian coffees are now trademarked in more than 30 countries and income for the coffee sector in Ethiopia has increased by $100 million. Layton recently visited a coffee farming region in Ethiopia and saw first-hand the changes brought about by the increased income. "It was very clear that the coffee farmers were considerably better off than they had been. Some of them had built roofs on their houses and sent their kids to school for the first time. Physically you could see the change that the project has brought to their lives," he said.

The organization currently has more than a dozen projects in 14 countries. In addition to the coffee sector in Ethiopia, Light Years has worked with producers of Darjeeling Tea in India, chocolate in Ghana, and tequila in Mexico. There is a strong component of local involvement to ensure the suitability and sustainability of the intellectual property strategy. "We actually go to the countries and talk to the stakeholders there. Together they develop a strategy, consult stakeholders and the government, and then it is implemented," said Light Years Accounts Manager Antonnete Namai.

Recently, Light Years partnered with the Natural Resources Institute to conduct a series of intellectual property workshops in Mozambique and Kenya to promote awareness of intellectual property and its significance and to equip entrepreneurs with the tools to take control of the intangible value of their products, and with it, their futures. —Zenah Hasan

Restoring Hope for the Future

It was a chance encounter with a Mercy Ships volunteer in 2005 that changed Harris' life forever. The 34-year-old Liberian fisherman had lived with a nearly basketball-sized tumor on his face for 13 years. Besides causing other villagers to shun Harris, the six pound tumor was slowly suffocating him. But when a Mercy Ships volunteer stopping in Harris' village heard about the man with the deformed face, he sought him out and brought him to the ship for surgery. Today, Harris lives a normal life with virtually no sign of the tumor that haunted him for years.

Harris is just one of the many people who have had their lives, and their futures, changed forever when a Mercy Ship docked near their home, bringing state-of-the art hospital facilities and highly trained medical professionals to their front door. Mercy Ships was founded in 1978 by Don and Deyon Stephens, who borrowed $1 million to transform a retired cruise ship into a modern, floating hospital that could fulfill their dream of bringing life-transforming medical care to the world's poor. The Anastasis was the first of four hospital ships that have provided care in Africa, Asia and South America.

Mercy Ships staff provides a range of medical and surgical procedures that are generally unavailable in developing countries, most commonly maxillofacial procedures to correct benign tumors and other facial deformities, cleft palates repair, cataract removal, the repair of obstetric vaginal fistulas, and orthopedic corrections. Since 1978, Mercy Ships has performed more than 1.7 million services valued at over $670 million and helped more than 1.9 million people.

Today, Mercy Ships operates its state-of-the-art flagship hospital ship Africa Mercy in the coastal waters of West Africa, deploying to various locations for 10-month tours of duty. It is the only nongovernmental hospital ship in Africa. The ship is staffed by 450 medical and nonmedical volunteers from 35 different countries, who pay their own way to ensure that donations to Mercy Ships are maximized for patient care. Mercy Ships, a US-based PVO, operates on an annual budget of $32 million. It receives its funding primarily from individuals and foundations, and some funding from the U.S. Agency for International Development. A total of 82% of Mercy Ships budget is dedicated to its programs, while 8% goes to administration and 10% to fundraising.

Mercy Ships' work goes beyond providing much-needed medical care to helping with long-term development in the countries it visits. Mercy Ships builds schools, trains medical personnel and provides community health education. It also provides teams of agricultural and sanitation experts to work with local villages to build or maintain community water and sanitation facilities and agricultural projects. To date, it has taught more than 14,500 local healthcare and professional workers, who have in turn trained many others in primary health care, and has completed more than 900 community development projects, including construction of schools, clinics, orphanages, wells and agriculture programs. In recognition of its work, Mercy Ships' founders were awarded with Variety International's Humanitarian of the Year Award in 2009.

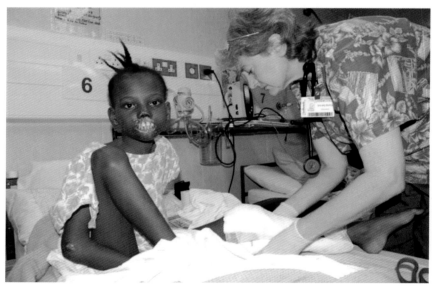

Mercy Ships brings state-of-the art medical facilities to coastal countries in West Africa, providing surgeries that are usually unavailable, including correction of maxillofacial deformities and benign tumors.

But beyond medical care and clean water and schools, what Mercy Ships brings is hope in the future. "I can see hope come back into the eyes of fathers and mothers when they look at their children. Hope that they will have a future," says Chief Medical Officer Dr. Gary Parker.   —Yan Zhang

Universities and Colleges: $1.7 Billion

Americans continue to be generous in their support for international students. The CGP used data from the Institute for International Education's annual *Open Doors* survey to determine that Americans gave a total of $1.7 billion in support to students from the developing world in the 2008-2009 academic year, a slight increase from the 2007–2008 adjusted total of $1.6 billion. Among the sources of funds are the U.S. colleges and universities and other private sponsors, such as foundations, businesses, and religious organizations. More than a quarter of the foreign students studying in the U.S. report that the primary source of funding for their education is their U.S. college or university, a private sponsor, or an international organization.

The United States continues to welcome students from the developing world. The number of international students at universities and colleges in the United States increased by 7.7% to a record high of 671,616 in the 2008–2009 academic year. According to data from *Open Doors*, 61%, or 410,712, of international students in the 2008–2009 academic year came to the United States from developing countries. Of this group, 66% came from Asia and the Pacific, 16% came from Latin America, 8% came from sub-Saharan Africa, 6% from Europe and Central Asia, and 3% from North Africa and the Middle East.

According to *Open Doors*, India was the number one country of origin for international students studying in the United States in the 2008–2009 academic year, displacing China, last year's leader. Of the 671,616 international students, 15.4% came from India, 14.6% from China and 11.2% from South Korea. Canada and Japan rounded out the top five countries of origin for international students studying in the United States. Students from these five countries accounted for 50% of all international students in the United States. Of the international students enrolled, 59% were enrolled in doctoral programs. California, New York, Texas, Massachusetts and Florida were the top five states attracting international students, accounting for 39% of the total.

Today's college and university students are a global, service-oriented generation. Some colleges and universities, however, instill an international service ethic that carries on through graduating class after class, as demonstrated by the Peace Corps annual ranking of the top colleges and universities that produce the most Peace Corps volunteers. According to the Peace Corps, the University of Washington is the large college or university (more than 15,000 undergraduates) that currently produces the most Peace Corps volunteers, with 101 volunteers serving around the world, followed by the University of Colorado at Boulder with 95 and the University of California–Berkley with 89. The University of California–Berkley holds the all-time Peace Corp volunteer record, having produced 3,412 volunteers.[17]

The George Washington University leads among medium-sized colleges and universities (5,000–15,000 undergraduates), producing 53 current Peace Corp volunteers, followed by American University with 51 volunteers

> The University of Washington currently produces the most Peace Corp volunteers, with 101 volunteers serving around the world. The University of California–Berkley holds the all-time Peace Corp volunteer record.

and Cornell University with 46. St. Olaf College leads among small colleges and universities (less than 5,000 undergraduates), producing 26 volunteers, followed by the University of Mary Washington with 23 and Middlebury College with 21.[18]

"Peace Corps service is a life changing leadership opportunity and a great career foundation in almost every field, ranging from international development, education, public health, engineering, agriculture, and law, to name a few. I am proud of our historic relationship with over 3,000 colleges and universities in the United States and look forward to recruiting and training the next generation of Peace Corps volunteers," said Peace Corps Director Aaron S. Williams.[19]

THE NOOTBAAR INSTITUTE ON LAW, RELIGION AND ETHICS

Justice for the World

Overburdened and understaffed, Uganda's criminal justice system fights to keep up in a country with a not-too-distant history of civil war and internal strife. Individuals charged with a crime are known to wait in jail anywhere from seven months to seven years for their first hearing, causing terrible overcrowding. The lack of resources and organization hampers the country's quest to move forward.

When students from Pepperdine University's Herbert and Elinor Nootbaar Institute on Law, Religion and Ethics arrived at Uganda's Criminal Court to help modernize the country's judicial system, they found a passion for progress amidst a sea of chaos. "All of the cases from 1979 and before were crammed floor-to-ceiling in a dank closet," said student Greer Illingworth.

Over the past year, ten students from the Nootbaar Institute's Global Justice Program worked to help organize Uganda's judicial system to increase its efficiency and improve the nation's rule of law. Students have organized the backlog of case files and created an indexing system. They also worked with Google Books to archive the information on the Internet.

Thanks to a $6 million endowment from Elinor and Herbert Nootbaar, Pepperdine University Law School's Institute on Law, Religion, and Ethics Law has been able to expand its Global Justice Program. The Nootbaars became supporters of Pepperdine because they strongly identify with the school's

The Nootbaar Institute at Pepperdine University worked with Uganda's criminal court to help modernize the country's judicial system.

mission to train students to be service minded and purpose driven. "When we realized the extent of their work and the programs and mission, we were so inspired that we wanted to help," Elinor Nootbaar said.

The Global Justice Program enables law students to gain practical experience through international internship placements with human rights organizations. As part of the program, students have assisted in combating human trafficking in Thailand, worked to protect religious freedom in Eastern Europe, and served as law clerks to the High Court in Uganda. During his time in Uganda, Illingworth was asked by the head of the Criminal Court to help write a judicial opinion for a prisoner who had been convicted of robbery four years earlier. Working on the case with other Pepperdine students, Illingworth came to the conclusion that the prisoner had been wrongfully convicted. The students' judicial opinion was successfully used in court and saved the man from spending the next 18 months of his life in prison.

"The program has made an incredible impact in the countries we work in," said Jay Milbrandt, Director of the Global Justice Program. "The students have been able to suggest and implement legal concepts into developing judicial systems that will change the way these countries provide legal services to the poor." For example, Illingworth and other students suggested that Uganda implement plea bargaining—a practice Uganda did not have—to improve judicial expediency and docket management. After they presented their suggestion to the principal judge, the judiciary decided to implement the tool in the country's court system.

The Nootbaar Institute is working to ensure the longevity of the program through partnerships with international organizations, such as the International Justice Mission and Saddleback Church. The Pepperdine School of Law has signed a Memorandum of Understanding with the Ugandan Judiciary to continue and expand its relationship with the country as the law school and the Nootbaar Institute work to create lasting change in one of the world's most vulnerable places.

—Emma Britz

University of Washington Business School
The Noble Purpose of Business

From a plan to set up mobile dental units in rural India to a blueprint to produce pedal-powered phones in Nicaragua, today's business students are using their entrepreneurial drive to solve the world's problems. Each year, the University of Washington's (UW) Global Social Entrepreneurship Competition helps students turn some of these plans into reality.

The global competition, held annually in Seattle by UW's Global Business Center, had a modest beginning in 2005 with seven teams representing five countries. In 2009, the competition drew 70 entries from 16 countries. This competition is set to become a critical platform for incubating the next generation of social entrepreneurs who are driven to address some of the world's most pressing social problems and to provide creative new methods to solve these problems. What sets their ideas apart from others with a similar desire to solve the world's problems is their commercial sustainability, a key criterion of the competition.

Over the course of a week, 16 teams selected from 70 applicants are matched with mentors drawn from the local and international business community who will help them polish their business plans and introduce them to industry experts. At the end of the week, the teams have 10 minutes to convince a panel of judges from the public and private sector of their ability to organize capital, deliver the product or service, impact the community and negotiate with government regulators. Four finalists compete the following day to take away the $10,000 grand prize sponsored by the Microsoft Corporation and two prizes sponsored by the University of Washington Department of Global Health.

While winning teams take away the prize money, the non-winning finalists are not losers, as the competition generates valuable publicity for their projects. "The Global Social Entrepreneurship Competition was our very first business competition and a launch pad for our future endeavors. The skills we gained—from learning how to fine-tune our presentation and pitch to investors to gaining access to market contacts— were highly beneficial," said Chris Meyer, of Plantation Empowerment, a 2007 finalist whose sustainable timber project was later implemented in Panama. "The credibility and experience allowed us to do well in other competitions, raising more than $10,000 in capital for our venture," he added.

Young entrepreneurs participating in the University of Washington's Global Social Entrepreneurship Competition compete to have their social entrepreneurship project funded.

In fact, competition finalists have a strong track record of getting financing for their plans. "Out of 10 to 14 business proposals, we have seen one or two business ideas implemented each year," says Wren McNally, assistant director of faculty and community programs at the UW Global Business Center/Foster School of Business.

The 2009 grand prize winning team, Aahar, from the Narsee Monjee Institute of Management Studies in India, hopes to follow in that winning tradition. The team designed an 800-calorie, ready-to-eat meal manufactured from rice, lentils, unrefined sugar and vegetables, including vegetable peels discarded by food processors. The meals will be sold for 5 rupees (about 10 cents) to residents of Mumbai's largest slum to combat widespread hunger and malnutrition. The business proposes to double its impact by employing local women at wages higher than generally available in the slum.

The team is currently pursuing investors and hopes to implement the business within a year of graduating. The 2008 grand prize winning team, KAITE, an innovative organic farming initiative for small farmers in Zimbabwe, is already operational.

"The Global Social Entrepreneurship Competition gets to the noble purpose of business," said James Jiambaivo, the dean of the UW Foster School of Business, but most of the competitors would say it is just good business.—**Ai Gee Ong**

Building Tomorrow
Students for Students

Most people might not think there is much they could do about the fact that only 57% of Ugandan children finish primary school. But when American student George Srour visited Uganda in 2004 as a United Nations intern, he came back to the United States determined to make a difference for some of the world's most vulnerable children. In the following four months, he and his fellow students at the College of William & Mary raised an astounding $45,000 to build a school in Kampala, Uganda. When Srour won the William E. Simon Fellowship for Noble Purpose in 2005, which recognizes graduating seniors committed to service, he turned his vision of providing education to those in need into a full-time avocation and founded Building Tomorrow.

Building Tomorrow empowers students to raise funds to build schools in Uganda. It provides college and high school students with resources, expertise and organizational support to help them to sponsor fundraising activities at their schools. The nonprofit organization, which is based in Srour's home state of Indiana, identifies areas in Uganda where children have poor access to primary schools, buys a plot of land, and, using the money raised by students in the United States, works with the local community to construct a 10-room schoolhouse. The completed school is leased to the local government, which manages day-to-day operations. Since the original school in Kampala, which is now educating 350 students, Building Tomorrow has completed four additional schools that are teaching almost 900 students.

Building Tomorrow currently has 17 college chapters and a partnership with Key Club International, the world's largest high school service organization, and continues to add new chapters. Srour says the organization is expanding because there is "a growing culture of people wanting to be involved with this kind of work." He notes that because college chapters are directly linked to a specific school, with some students

even going to visit the site, "there's a tangible link that people have when they take part in raising funds to build a school."

But Building Tomorrow isn't simply about raising money in the United States and sending it to Uganda. There's a strong link between the local Ugandan population and organization. Part of what decides the location of a school is the willingness of the local community to provide the 25,000 hours of labor that is required for the school to be built. "Everyone realizes that they have a hand in educating these kids. That's where we're trying to create kind of a culture shift: traditionally, parents have not had a very active role in education," says Srour.

All on-campus donations to Building Tomorrow go directly to building schools; administrative costs are covered by a variety of grants and donations. This, says Srour, is another factor in the success of the project, as students feel that their donations are making a difference and are encouraged to give more. In addition, as part of its commitment to universal primary education, the Ugandan Ministry of Education has agreed to provide teachers for each of the schools funded by Building Tomorrow.

Seven-year-old Ventril is one of the children whose life was changed by Building Tomorrow. Before a school was built in his community, the nearest school was two and a half hours away. Now Ventril is among the 325 children enrolled in the Building Tomorrow Academy of Lutisi, the first step in fulfilling his dream of becoming an engineer. —Eimear O'Leary-Barrett

Religious Organizations: $8.2 Billion

The CGP has continued its groundbreaking work on U.S. giving for international relief and development by U.S. congregations with a new survey for *Index 2010* measuring giving in 2008. This year, the Urban Institute's National Center on Charitable Statistics teamed up with the Social and Economic Sciences Research Center at Washington State University to conduct a national survey on congregational support for international giving and relief. Combined with data from the Billy Graham Center on giving by Protestant mission agen-

Schoolchildren outside the newly opened Academy of Kiyamba in Uganda. Building Tomorrow has raised funds to build four schools in Uganda.

Talia Leman: Harnessing the Compassion of Children

Talia Leman has accomplished more in charitable works by age 14 than most can brag about in a lifetime. Founder and CEO of RandomKid.org, a site that connects and supports children from around the world in their philanthropic efforts, Talia has inspired thousands of youth to believe in their ability to change the world.

Talia's efforts began in the wake of the Hurricane Katrina disaster in 2005 when she was just 10 years old. Profoundly moved by the events she saw taking place on the news, Talia was compelled to do something. She began by emailing everyone she knew, asking for donations. What started as a swelling of sympathy in the heart of a child became a nationwide movement. Talia and her network of peers raised $10 million dollars for Katrina relief.

Shortly thereafter, Talia founded RandomKid.org to harness the power of children's philanthropic efforts and to inspire children around the world to tackle big issues—both locally and globally. "I started it to show the world the power of anyone to solve real world problems," Talia told a group of Girl Scouts in one of her many appearances to motive youth to become involved in philanthropy. Beyond mobilizing youth,

the organization provides hands-on assistance with project development, interest free microloans to start projects, and assistance with web site design, public relations and finances.

In 2008, RandomKid.org pooled the resources of children from the United States and 20 other countries to raise money to open a school in rural Cambodia that now serves 400 children. In a speech at the school's opening, Talia explained why she is so passionate about education for all of the world's children: "When we grow up, we are going to need all of us to make the world what it needs to be. We will need your skills, your talents, your energy and your knowledge to make the world the best place it can be."

In addition to numerous domestic projects, the organization has raised money to drill wells in Africa and to provide mosquito nets to prevent malaria in the developing world.

Talia has been the recipient of numerous international and national awards for her philanthropic work, including being named UNICEF's National Youth Ambassador and Youth Spokesperson in 2005–2006. She was a recipient of a World of Children Award,

Fourteen-year-old Talia Leman founded RandomKid.org to inspire children to come together to tackle the world's big problems.

popularly known as the "Nobel Prize for Children," in 2008 for her work to improve the lives of the world's children

Talia's story is a celebration of the power and creativity of each individual to affect change in his or her world. However, she knows that this can only come with hard work and dedication. She is adamant that kids remain true to themselves, employing their methods, styles, and ideas. Talia believes passionately that it is today's children who have the big ideas to solve tomorrow's problems. "Believe in your dreams," she says. "You have the power in you to make this world a better place!" —Emily Gikow

---

cies and data from the Church of Jesus Christ of Latter Day Saints, the *Index* continues to provide a unique look at overall international relief and development giving by U.S. religious institutions. Research by CGP's partners shows that religious giving totaled $8.2 billion in 2008, up $200 million from a revised 2007 total of $8 billion.

Historically, religious giving tends to be among the most resilient of all forms of charitable giving in times of economic hardship.[20] Approximately 50% of congregations surveyed by the Congregational Economic Impact Study reported an increase in fundraising between 2007 and 2008. Also, nearly

37% of congregations responding to the survey said fundraising increased in the first half of 2009 compared to 2008, while 29% reported a decrease.[21] As with other philanthropic organizations, religious congregations report they are trying new fundraising strategies, merging programs or operations with other congregations and reducing operating costs in response to the recession.[22]

The response to the Haiti earthquake illustrated the continued importance of religious organizations to overseas relief and development efforts. Two organizations featured in this year's *Index*, Catholic Relief Services and American

Jewish World Service, are involved in Haiti relief efforts. Other faith-based groups involved in relief include Baptist Haiti Mission, Episcopal Relief & Development, Samaritan's Purse, The Salvation Army, the United Methodist Committee on Relief, World Concern, and WorldVision.

CATHOLIC RELIEF SERVICES
Made in the Shade

Once upon a time the hills surrounding Port-de-Paix in northwest Haiti teemed with coffee trees. The abundant coffee crop made the area a major center for the coffee trade. But when the price of coffee plummeted in the late 1980s, the area's coffee crop withered, along with its economy. Today the rural region is one of the poorest in Haiti. The loss of coffee trees from the hillsides has also accelerated deforestation, making the area vulnerable to mudslides during punishing tropical rains.

But thanks to an innovative partnership rooted in the area's Catholic tradition, coffee is making a comeback in Port-de-Paix. Catholic Relief Services (CRS), the international humanitarian agency of the U.S. Catholic Church, and the Archdiocese of Miami are working with the local Catholic Church and international partners on a fair trade coffee project designed to restore sustainable coffee farming to Port-de-Paix. Other partners in the project are St. Thomas University in Miami, the Just Trade Center, and Pascucci Torrefazione, a leading Italian specialty coffee roaster.

At the initiative of Bishop Pierre-Antoine Paulo, the bishop of Port-de-Paix, local residents created a coffee cooperative to bring coffee farming back to the region. Today the 200 members of the Cafeiere et Cacouyere du Nord'Quest (COCANO) cooperative grow Cafe Cocano, a fair trade, organic, shade grown coffee. Members of the cooperative sell the processed beans directly to Pascucci Torrefazione, which ensures a sustainable living for families in the area.

Catholic Relief Services has provided financial support to the project through its Fair Trade Fund, which provides high-impact grants to artisans and farmers to launch Fair Trade projects. A grant of $15,000 from CRS allowed the cooperative to hire an expert from the Just Trade Center to help them establish the cooperative and assist with long-term planning.

CRS has also committed $15,000 to St. Thomas University to provide marketing support to the project. Jacqueline De Carlo, senior program advisor for economic justice at CRS, says that the organization hopes to "help build the capacity for production of the coffee, help keep the production and sale fair-trade, and increase the number of customers."

In 2008, the cooperative sold 35,000 pounds of coffee beans and in 2009 it harvested its second batch of beans. Anthony Vinciguerra, director of the Center for Justice and Peace at St. Thomas University, which is providing marketing support for the project, said, "The initiative has worked so well because Port-de-Paix has a long history of coffee production" and local farmers still have the knowledge of how to produce good coffee. Vinciguerra notes that the initiative is designed to promote long-term, sustainable development in the local communities. "The farmers do not want to be controlled by foreigners," he said, which is why they have full ownership of the project and are in charge of everything they produce and sell.

The recent devastating earthquake in Haiti has made the fair trade coffee initiative more important than ever, according to Vinciguerra, as refugees from devastated Port-au-Prince have streamed into rural areas like Port-de-Paix, which makes rebuilding rural economies and promoting development crucial. "The coffee cooperative is bringing hope for long-term development in the region. There are challenges of course but we are lucky to have partners like CRS working with us through this difficult time," he said.

—Zivile Gedrimaite

HOPE INTERNATIONAL
Spreading Seeds of Self-Sufficiency

Jeff Rutt traveled to Zaporozhye, Ukraine in 1997 with his local church, bearing containers of food, clothing, and medical supplies. Seeing the great need in the country, the church's generosity expanded to include the purchase of a sunflower seed oil press, which, the church hoped, the town would use to initiate a small business. The venture languished, however, and the sunflower press remained untouched. A pastor in the community told Rutt the church's charity had created

His experience in the Ukraine led Rutt to the concept of microfinance, with its promise of building self-sufficiency through economic development. He decided to marry microfinance with a faith-based development PVO.

an unhealthy dependence on American aid and suppressed local businesses; he said that what the citizens of Zaporozhye needed was a hand up, not a hand out.

His experience in the Ukraine inspired Rutt to seek a better solution to combat poverty, which led him to the concept of microfinance, with its promise of building self-sufficiency through economic development. He decided to marry microfinance with a faith-based development PVO. Thirteen years later, the organization he founded, HOPE International, is a leading Christian nonprofit network of microfinance institutions operating in 14 countries and supporting 250,000 entrepreneurs worldwide.

HOPE, headquartered in Lancaster, PA, partners a belief in the potential of microfinance to lift individuals out of poverty with a belief that economic development goes beyond income and touches on moral values. HOPE offers small business loans, savings services, and biblically based business training and mentoring that emphasize good business practices in the context of Christian ethics. According to Ken Tordoff, director of marketing for HOPE, "Biblically-based business training integrates scripture into the teaching and explanation of responsibilities and ethics, such as the paying back of loans and how to treat clients' customers."

Loans range from $50 to $2,000. The loan staff consists of indigenous employees who are familiar with the local context. While most of the organization's employees are Christians, HOPE is a non-denominational organization that serves clients regardless of religious affiliation. The organization targets underserved countries where financial services are least available and economic innovation is difficult. It is active in the Democratic Republic of Congo, Burundi, Dominican Republic, Haiti, Moldova, Romania, and Russia.

HOPE's business model has been extremely successful; the organization has a 99% repayment rate. In 2008, HOPE distributed $80 million in loans, with over 350,000 individual loans granted. HOPE raised approximately $6.5 million in 2009. The main sources of HOPE's funding are individuals and foundations. HOPE spends less than 15% of its funds on administrative expenses and fundraising. It is a member of the Evangelical Council for Financial Accountability and has been consistently recognized by Charity Navigator as an excellent steward of donor resources.

As a network-based organization, HOPE partners with local microfinance organizations in each community. Tordoff says this is important because "in each country there are different forms of ownership and investment by HOPE; in some countries HOPE is a partner and others they own 100% outright."

As HOPE continues to grow its network of microfinance organizations, it has also worked to change the role and work of churches back home in the United States. HOPE recently published *Perspectives for Global Poverty*, a study guide designed to educate and inform evangelicals in the United States about poverty and ways to alleviate poverty other than through charity. —**Andrew Baltes**

AMERICAN JEWISH WORLD SERVICE
To Save One Life

When three-year-old Kadijat became ill suddenly, her parents in the remote Nigerian village of Mazakuka feared the worst. They could not afford to take her to the health facility and relied on home remedies that were not working. "I thought my daughter was going to die," said her father. "She vomited repeatedly until there was nothing left in her stomach…I watched her rapidly going down before my very eyes."

Kadijat did not die, however, thanks to a Nigerian PVO called Physicians for Social Justice, which arrived in Mazakuka five days into her illness to provide free medical services to the community. A physician diagnosed malaria and administered $3 worth of anti-malarial treatment at no cost to her family. Her father called the visit of the Physicians for Social Justices mobile health team "a miracle."

Physicians for Social Justice is improving health care for rural Nigerians thanks to a grant from American Jewish World Service, an international development organization estab-

Through American Jewish World Service, children in rural Nigeria receive anti-malarial medicine.

than $13 million to PVOs in 36 countries in Asia, Africa and the Americas. American Jewish World Service began its partnership with Physicians for Social Justice, a community-based development organization active in 10 poor rural communities in Nigeria, in 2007 with a grant of $21,500. Physicians for Social Justice has used the grant money to reduce the high child mortality rate from malaria in Nigeria's remote Mashegu region, where malaria accounts for 30% of deaths of children under five and 40% of healthcare costs for local families. It is providing malaria-prevention education, distributing insecticide-treated bed nets, and providing life-saving medical care.

lished in Boston in 1985 by a group of rabbis, Jewish community leaders, businesspeople, and scholars. It is dedicated to alleviating poverty, hunger and disease across the globe. The organization works with grassroots organizations to improve civil society and promote sustainable development and human rights, while promoting volunteerism and philanthropy within the Jewish community. "We are of a faith that reminds us daily of our responsibility, of our need to act, of our need to help save some or any one of these children. We are taught that to save one life is to save the world," says Ruth Messinger, president of the organization.

In 2008, the organization made 488 grants totaling more

With support from American Jewish World Service, Physicians for Social Justice estimates it improved the health status of more than 24,500 children in 2008. The project also provided more than 7,000 young people in eight rural secondary schools with life skills education and HIV/AIDS prevention education.

The success of the project is due to the ability of Physicians for Social Justice to do a great deal of good with a small amount of money. According to its president, Dr. Ibrahim Idris, "For another child, $1 may be worth just a candy, but for a 4-year-old girl dying of malaria in rural Mashegu, $1 is worth her life."

—Jason M. Farrell

1   Steven Lawrence, "Foundations' Year-end Outlook for Giving and the Sector," Foundation Center, November 2009, http://foundationcenter.org/gainknowledge/research/pdf/researchadvisory_economy_200911.pdf (accessed February 3, 2010).

2   The Foundation Center, *International Grantmaking IV: An Update on U.S. Foundation Trends*, New York: The Foundation Center, 2008.

3   Ibid.

4   Committee Encouraging Corporate Philanthropy, *Giving in Numbers 2009*, CECP, 2009.

5   Caroline Preston, "Corporate Leaders Tout Philanthropy's Benefits Amid Grim Financial News," *The Chronicle of Philanthropy*, Feb. 24, 2009.

6   Ibid.

7   Ibid.

8   2009 Corporate Volunteer International Forum held in Beijing, http://www.csr360gpn.org/news/story/2009-corporate-volunteer-international-

forum-held-in-beijing (accessed March 5, 2010).

9   Inyoung Hwang, "Foreign aid suffers as financial crisis persists," ipiu.com, http://upiu.com/articles/foreign-aid-suffers-as-financial-crisis-persists (accessed March 1, 2010).

10 Ibid.

11 Katherine Baldwin, "Aid agencies discuss funding shortfall, 2010 outlook," Reuters, Dec. 21, 2009.

12 "Less money for more work–the NGO double whammy," irin.com, http://www.irinnews.org/Report.aspx?ReportId=84023 (accessed March 1, 2010).

13 Michael Zielenziger, "From Job Loss to Peace Corps," *AARP Bulletin*, Sept. 16, 2009.

14 Stephanie Chen, "More older Americans signing on to volunteer abroad," CNN.com, April 23, 2009.

15 Travelocity, "Travel for Good," http://www.travelocity.com/TravelForGood/voluntourism.html (accessed Feb. 23, 2010).

16 Ibid.

17 Peace Corps Top Colleges 2010, http://multimedia.peacecorps.gov/multimedia/pdf/stats/schools2010.pdf.

18 Ibid.

19 Peace Corps Announces Top College and University Rankings, Peace Corps press release, Feb. 4, 2010.

20 The Lake Institute on Faith & Giving and the Center on Philanthropy at Indiana University, "Religious Giving in Uncertain times: Insights for Congregations and Faith-based Nonprofits," Nov. 20, 2008, http://www.ucc.org/stewardship/faith-and-tough-econmic-times/Lake-Institute-Religious-Giving-in-Uncertain-Times-11-21-08.pdf (accessed March 5, 2010).

21 Lake Institute on Faith and Giving and the Alban Institute, *Congregational Economic Impact Study*, http://www.philanthropy.iupui.edu/Lake-FamilyInstitute/docs/2009CongregationalEconomicImpactStudy.pdf (accessed March 5, 2010).

22 Ibid.

Former Irish Prime Minister Bertie Ahern greets residents of the impoverished Tafelsig area of South Africa, where the Niall Mellon Township Trust is building 500 houses for residents who live in shacks.

INTERNATIONAL PHILANTHROPY OUTSIDE OF THE UNITED STATES

Giving Goes Global

Private philanthropy is on the upswing around the world, as entrenched ways of giving make room for the more dynamic and accountable types of philanthropy that have found favor in the United States. As this section will demonstrate, there has been a notable increase in foundations across Europe and a surge of giving in India and China. The so-called BRIC (the emerging economies of Brazil, Russia, India and China) countries have seen the emergence of robust philanthropic sectors (see box page 44). As in the United States, an entrepreneurial donor class is emerging throughout Europe and young Europeans are emulating their counterparts across the Atlantic and giving directly to chosen charities, eschewing the typical European pattern of giving primarily through taxes. There is also increasing cross-pollination between U.S. and European philanthropists and growing interest in strategic philanthropy and social investment.

Despite greater attention to philanthropy in Europe and Asia, measuring non-U.S. private giving from developed countries continues to have its challenges. Although Development Assistance Committee (DAC) member governments report their overseas private giving to the Organiza-

tion for Economic Co-operation and Development (OECD) on an annual basis, these figures are incomplete and in some cases nonexistent. The numbers are largely based on voluntary surveys of PVOs that do not capture all PVO donations. Nor do developed country donors fully report giving by corporations, foundations, religious organizations and volunteer contributions.

This edition of the *Index of Global Philanthropy and Remittances* is able to provide a more comprehensive picture of private philanthropy from developed countries other than the United States to the developing world than previously available. With the addition of Italy and Switzerland since the last edition, the *Index* now reports improved private giving number for 13 developed countries other than the

United States: Denmark, Finland, France, Italy, Luxembourg, the Netherlands, New Zealand, Norway, Portugal, Spain, Sweden, Switzerland and the United Kingdom.

The 13 countries for which the Center for Global Prosperity (CGP) was able to compile more complete numbers reported total private giving of only $1.5 billion to the OECD in 2008. CGP research partners, however, found $10.3 billion for these same 13 countries for 2008. When combined with the other eight donors, CGP found that non-U.S. private philanthropy amounted to $15.3 billion. This is a 25% increase (not accounting for inflation) compared to $12.2 billion in 2007.

To obtain our private giving estimate for the United Kingdom, CGP again partnered with GuideStar Data Services (GDS). Total private UK giving to the developing world

through UK charities working in overseas aid/famine relief amounted to $6.3 billion. This assessment of UK private giving excludes foundations, corporations and churches, so the actual total is certainly higher. It is also far higher than the $462 million in overseas private giving that the UK government reported to the OECD for 2008.[1]

To obtain our private giving estimate for France, the CGP obtained an update on French individual giving to developing countries for 2008 and combined it with 2007 data on French corporate giving, the most recent year for which these data were available.

French private sources gave $1.0 billion in 2008 to developing countries. This includes $468.6 million from individuals, $33.5 million from bequests, and $502.5 million from corporations. To obtain our private giving estimate for Italy, the CGP partnered with Instituto per la Riceraca Sociale (IRS), an independent, non-profit research organization based in Italy. IRS collected data from Italian PVOs that worked in international aid in 2008, as well as a number of Italian banking foundations that make substantial contributions to the developing world. In total, the IRS estimates $583.1 million in Italian private giving to the developing world, substantially more than the $105 million reported by the Italian government to the OECD.[2]

The private giving estimate for Spain is based on a report by Coordinadora ONG Para El Desarrollo España, a Spanish association of 100 international development organizations, which estimated $409.2 million in Spanish private giving to the developing world in 2007, the most recent year for which data are available. This includes $170.4 million in regular donations and fees; $140.2 million in one-time donations; $47.5 million from private enterprises; $34.4 million from the sale of fair trade products and merchandising; and $16.7 million from other private funds. Spain does not report any private giving to OECD.

The private giving estimate for Portugal is based on a survey of large Portuguese PVOs conducted by CGP staff using Plataforma Portuguesa das ONGD, the largest Portuguese international development organization umbrella group, as a resource. The CGP determined that Portuguese PVOs received $9.0 million in private contributions in 2007. The figure is conservative due to the lack of reporting by the majority of PVOs and foundations in Portugal and the lack of sources for corporate and religious giving. It is still significantly higher, however, than the $1 million in private overseas giving reported by the Portuguese government to the OECD.[3]

Center for Global Prosperity staff surveyed 62 of the largest members of Le Cercle de Coopération des ONG de Développement, the only international development PVO umbrella group in Luxembourg. The CGP was able to establish private giving numbers for 16 of the organizations, totaling $19.6 million in private giving to the developing world from Luxembourg. Luxembourg reported $11 million in private giving for 2008 to the OECD.[4]

The private giving estimate for the Netherlands is based on the 2009 edition of the biannual report *Geven in Nederland* produced by the Vrije Universiteit Amsterdam, which provides data for 2007, the most recent year for which data are available. According to the report, households gave

$399.4 million to international aid causes in cash and in-kind donations; $54.9 million came from bequests; $22.8 million came from foundations; $93.8 million came from corporate gifts and sponsorship; and $126.0 million came from lotteries, for a total of $696.9 million in Dutch private giving to the developing world. The Dutch government reported $330 million in private giving for 2008 to the OECD.[5]

To obtain private giving estimates for the Scandinavian countries and Switzerland, CGP partnered with Stein Brothers AB, a Swedish research and consulting firm. Stein Brothers collected data on Danish international giving in 2008

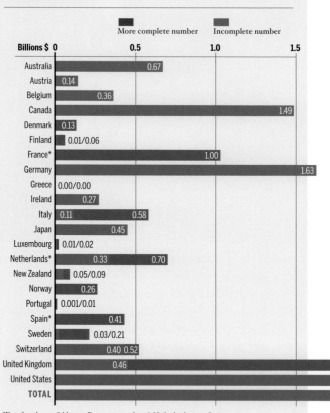

Figure 1

Incomplete Private Giving Numbers Submitted to OECD and More Complete Numbers from CGP, 2008 (Billions of $)

*Data from last available year: France, 2007 and 2008; Netherlands, 2007; Spain, 2007

Source: Stein Brothers, AB, Scandinavia 2009-2010; Charles Sellen, France, 2008-2009 and VU University Amsterdam Department of Philanthropy, Netherlands, 2009; Instituto per la Riceraca Sociale, Italy, 2009; Le Cercle de Cooperation des OND de Developpement, Annual Report, Luxenberg, 2009; Vrije Universiteit Amsterdam, Geven in Nederland 2009, Netherlands, 2009; Council on International Development, Annual Report, New Zealand, 2009; Plataforma Portuguesa das ONGD, Annual Report, Portugal, 2009; Coordinadora de ONG Para El Dessarrollo Espana, Informe de La Coordinadora de ONG Para El Desarrollo-Espana Sobre El Sector De Las ONGD, Spain, 2009; GuideStar Data Services, United Kingdom, 2009; Center for Global Prosperity, United States, 2009-2010 OECD.

Affluent European donors, mostly mid-to-late career professionals who have earned wealth through their own entrepreneurial initiatives, want to share that wealth and be involved in crafting solutions to society's pressing social problems.

in two areas: giving by international development PVOs and corporate giving. Danish private sources gave $133.7 million to the developing world: $120.4 million from PVOs and $13.3 million from one Danish multinational. The Danish government reported $129 million in private giving to the OECD.[6]

Stein Brothers collected data on Finnish international giving in 2008 in two areas: giving by international development PVOs and corporate giving. Private PVOs contributed $51.3 million in 2008, while corporate philanthropic contributions were $12.2 million, for a total of $63.5 million in Finnish private giving to the developing world. Finland reported a total of $13 million in private giving to the OECD.[7]

To obtain a private giving estimate for Norway, Stein Brothers measured giving by international development PVOs, for an estimated $261.6 million in private giving from Norwegian PVOs to the developing world in 2008. Norwegian corporations are assumed to be included in that figure because they give through PVOs. Norway did not report any private giving to the OECD in 2008.

To obtain private giving estimates for Sweden, Stein Brothers collected data on Swedish international giving in two areas: giving by international development PVOs and foundations and corporate giving. Swedish PVOs and foundations gave $177.2 million in 2008 to the developing world and Swedish companies gave $36.4 million for a total of $213.6

million in Swedish private giving to the developing world. The Swedish government reported $25 million in private giving to the OECD in 2008.[8]

To obtain private giving estimates for Switzerland, Stein Brothers collected data on Swiss international giving in two

areas: giving by international development PVOs and corporate giving. Swiss PVOs and foundations gave $438.0 million and Swedish companies gave $83.2 million to the developing world in 2008, for a total of $521.2 million in Swiss private giving to the developing world. The Swiss government reported $398 million in private giving to the OECD in 2008.[9]

The private giving number for New Zealand is based on data from the Council for International Development (CID), an umbrella body for New Zealand's major international development PVOs. According to CID's 2009 annual report, private income for its members came to $92.9 million in 2008: $85.0 million was from donations from the public and $7.9 million came from contracted work, foundation grants, grants from parent organizations, and the sale of goods. The New Zealand government reported $48 million in private giving to the OECD in 2008.[10]

PHILANTHROPY IN EUROPE

Until recently, the philanthropic landscape in Europe resembled the landscape in the United States several decades ago. It was dominated by a relatively small number of brand-name charities and large foundations created from the estates of the wealthy. Some of this still holds true. An analysis of 13 European Union countries (Belgium, Estonia, Finland, France, Germany, Hungary, Italy, Luxembourg, Slovenia, Slovakia, Spain, Sweden, and the UK) by the European Foundation Center found that in 2008 the top 10 foundations in these countries held almost one-quarter of foundation assets. In Luxembourg, Estonia, Slovenia and Finland, the top 15 foundations held more than 80% of total foundation assets.[11] However, that landscape is evolving rapidly as new players and new modes of giving enter the market. The same report by the European Foundation Center found that the number of public benefit foundations had increased by more than 50% between 2001 and 2005 to an estimated 95,000. In nine countries (Belgium, Estonia, France, Germany, Italy, Luxembourg, Slovakia, Spain and Sweden), 43% of foundations were created since 2001.[12]

In addition, a new generation of wealthy individual European donors is showing similar tendencies to its counterpart in the United States. Affluent European donors, mostly mid-to-late career professionals who have earned wealth through their own entrepreneurial initiatives, want to share that wealth and be involved in crafting solutions to society's

Divergent Paths: Philanthropy in BRIC Countries

In 2001, a Goldman Sachs economist coined the term BRIC to describe the world's four fastest growing developing economies: Brazil, Russia, India and China.[1] Today, the BRIC countries account for nearly 15% of the world's GDP and are expected to be a major force in the twenty-first century.[2] Apart from Russia, the BRIC countries are recipients of Official Development Assistance, and are also recipients of private philanthropy from OECD donor nations. These countries, however, are experiencing the growth of internal philanthropy, which provides a window into the development of emerging philanthropic sectors.

Philanthropy in Brazil stemmed from the Catholic Church, which supported nonprofit organizations that provided critical social services.[3] The secular nonprofit sector grew dramatically in the 1990s with the end of military rule and subsequent economic development. The growth of Brazil's business sector spurred growth in corporate philanthropy, which today dominates the philanthropic sector. The number of corporate foundations grew by 157% between 1996 and 2002. Fundacion Bradesco is Brazil's largest corporate foundation with $94 billion in assets. It has built 40 schools that provide a free, high-quality education to more than 700,000 poor, rural children.[4]

Individual philanthropy is less robust in Brazil. There are few tax incentives for individuals to make charitable donations and only limited options for setting up nonprofit organizations.[5] Organizations that study and promote best practices in philanthropy are on the rise. The Institute for the Development of Social Investment works to promote community-based philanthropic initiatives in Brazil.[6]

Philanthropy in Russia has been on the increase since 1990, shortly after the collapse of the Soviet Union. Corporate giving is estimated to have increased from $1 million annually in the early 1990s to some $2.5 billion annually today. Individual giving increased from almost nothing in the early 1990s to an official $20 million annually, although the actual amount is likely much higher.[7]

Most philanthropic activity in Russia is conducted by foundations established by wealthy oligarchs and by corporations. As of September 2008, Russia had more than 40 well-resourced private foundations. Corporate giving accounts for 60% of philanthropy in the country. However, almost half of this charity is linked to support of corporate "towns" established in the communist era.[8]

Most Russian individuals do not donate to PVOs because of widespread distrust of these organizations due to a series of scandals and the legacy of the communist era, when "charity" was banned.[9] As a result, while 60% of Russian individuals make charitable contributions, 90% of donations go to individuals or to state-run bodies such as orphanages and cultural institutions.[10] Current regulations in Russia provide little incentive for individual donors—donations to nonprofits are not tax deductible and individuals must go to a branch of the Savings Bank of Russia and fill out numerous forms to make even a small donation.[11]

The Russian government exerts considerable control over charitable giving and the nonprofit sector. The government channels philanthropy by soliciting contributions from the country's major philanthropists for a small number of chosen public infrastructure projects. Three-quarters of all philanthropists in Russia say they have been pressured by the government to support public works projects.[12] The Russian government has also cracked down on foundations that fund civil liberties projects. In 2006, the government froze the bank accounts of the Open

pressing social problems. A recent study of German foundations by the Bertelsmann Foundation found that 40% of foundation creators were under 60 years old and 43% founded their organization with funds earned through entrepreneurial activities.[13]

Philanthropy UK, a nonprofit founded by the UK government to provide information and resources to philanthropic donors, likewise identifies among its top ten trends in British philanthropy the emergence of a "new type of donor—one who is younger, typically (but not necessarily) self-made and socially conscious."[14] Still, the average middle-class European is more likely to make their philanthropic donations in cash to a neighborhood collector, much like the Christmas Salvation Army or Halloween UNICEF collections familiar to Americans.[15]

Many Europeans in countries such as Germany and all of Scandinavia also give through religious organizations in the form of church taxes. Under the church taxes, private citizens fund national churches, including their international charitable

Russia Foundation, a major foundation which promoted pro-democracy initiatives.[13] A 2006 law requiring all NGOs to re-register with the government and be audited was also seen as an attempt to limit the power of the nonprofit sector.[14]

In India, philanthropy is a longstanding tradition stemming from religious practices that encourage giving. Nationwide, 40% of all households in India give to charity and some 96% of upper and middle class households in urban regions donate money to charitable causes.[15, 16] Much giving in India is to churches or temples or in the form of in-kind donations, such as community food banks for the poor.

Corporate philanthropy is poorly tracked in India and even rough estimates are lacking. The most well known Indian corporate philanthropists are the founders of Tata Sons Limited, Ratan Tata and Dorabji Tata, who each started endowment funds that became the first national grantmaking foundations in India. The trusts fund educational institutions, cancer research, and projects in natural resource management, giving some $18 million annually.[17]

There has been concern in India over the lack of philanthropic involvement by newly wealthy business leaders.[18] There are four Indian billionaires on *Forbes'* list of the 10 wealthiest individuals in the world, but they have not distinguished themselves for philanthropy. Indian Prime Minister Manmohan Singh has urged corporate titans in that country to become involved in philanthropy.[19]

The Center for Advancement of Philanthropy in Mumbai encourages the growth of the nonprofit sector and acts as a liaison between Indian philanthropists and the government to promote partnerships.[20]

Philanthropy in China also stems from a cultural tradition of individual giving. Most donations are from wealthy individuals to local causes such as hospitals or disaster relief and overall levels of philanthropy are low. Total philanthropy in China amounts to .35% of GDP, compared to 2.1% in the United States.[21]

As in Russia, philanthropy in China is heavily regulated. The Chinese government allows only the China Red Cross and the Ministry of Civil Affairs to conduct fundraising activities for disaster relief. All non-profit organizations are regulated by the government and are called government operated nongovernmental organizations (GONGOs). These organizations are financed by the government and run by government staff.[22]

Corporations and wealthy individuals have started founding their own foundations, which donate through the GONGOs. In 2008, according to the Chinese Charity Donation Information Center, more than 1,500 foundations were registered in China. Privately owned businesses are the largest philanthropic donors in China, accounting for 43% of all domestic donations.[23]

The One Foundation started by Chinese-born actor Jet Li is the most well known Chinese foundation. It aggregates small donations—one yuan a month—from many individuals to encourage a culture of giving.[24] The foundation, which disperses funds through the Red Cross, raised more than $14 million for the victims of the Sichuan earthquake. The One Foundation has a transparent structure and utilizes innovative partnerships, such as a deal with China Merchants Bank for a credit card that will automatically debit a contribution to the foundation.[25]

The growing philanthropic sectors in the BRIC countries differ based on cultural traditions, attitudes about charity, and government regulation. In the more open societies of Brazil and India, a new philanthropic culture is free to flourish. The more authoritarian regimes of Russia and China have inhibited the growth of the philanthropic sector outside of strict government control. India and China have a long history of individual charity, but little tradition of giving to nonprofit organizations. Individual giving is constrained by cumbersome regulation in Brazil and Russia and none of the BRIC countries use the tax code to encourage giving. Billionaires in China and India have reaped huge fortunes in recent years but do not have a corporate giving culture, while Russian tycoons are pressured to contribute to the government's favored projects. However, foundations and think tanks in these countries are working to encourage a culture of philanthropy.

—Yulya Spantchak and Patti Miller

programs. But these funds are rarely considered "philanthropy" because they are collected as taxes rather than given directly.

The differences between Americans and Europeans in philanthropy are "beginning to level out," argues Wolfgang Hafenmeyer, Managing Partner at LGT Venture Philanthropy, the philanthropic fund of the Princely House of Liechtenstein. Hafenmeyer believes that the "high taxes–high services" argument for why European individuals have been less likely to give no longer applies to the younger generation.

"There is more cultural relativity today. More Europeans go to the United States to study, and wealthy families really live a global life—they have their money all over. Younger Europeans also have less faith in government and see a reason to engage in philanthropy," he says.[16]

There is also increasing cross-pollination between U.S. and European givers and social investors. For instance, A Glimmer of Hope, a young U.S. foundation which has been widely praised for its innovative approach to measurement and effectiveness in delivering community-based aid to Ethiopia, was founded by an Irish and English couple who emigrated to the United States because of their technology business. Similarly, The Children's Fund is a UK-based foundation tied to a major international hedge fund but run by the American wife of the hedge fund's manager. Scottish billionaire Tom Hunter has formed the Clinton Hunter Development Initiative, which is investing $100 million over 10 years in sustainable development programs in water and agriculture in conjunction with former U.S. President Bill Clinton.

PHILANTHROPY OUTSIDE THE U.S. AND THE RECESSION

The global economic crisis is having an effect on philanthropy outside of the United States just as it is in the United States. On average, European foundations' assets have dropped about 15–20%.[17] However, the impact of the recession has been muted in some European countries because there are fewer endowed foundations whose funds reside in the stock market, according to Judith Symonds, head of JCS International Philanthropy & Strategy Advisors.[18] Beatrice de Durfort of the French Centre of Foundations says there has not been a "major disaster" among French foundations.[19] A survey of attendees at the Coutts Forum for Philanthropy in the United Kingdom found that 87% intended to maintain or increase their level of charitable contributions in 2009.[20] And Germany has seen only a minor decline in general giving, says Michael Alberg-Seberich, executive partner at the Forum for Active Philanthropy in Berlin, adding, "Giving has proven remarkably recession proof."[21]

The consensus of participants in a recent forum in European philanthropy convened by *Alliance* magazine was that European foundations are trying to do "more with less." "What I'm seeing among my clients is a greater focus on what they're doing, which is very encouraging. A group of younger donors are really deciding they're going to mobilize their funds and work together to address certain issues. They are realizing they need to be more strategic, to pool funds and work together – and that is beginning to happen," says Judith Symonds.[22]

EUROPE AND STRATEGIC PHILANTHROPY

European philanthropists are embracing more engaged and strategic philanthropy. Among the elements of this strategic philanthropy are donors who are playing a more active role in identifying sectors and regions of interest; doing due diligence on potential recipients; and experimenting with alternative forms of financial assistance, such as loans and investment capital, in addition to grants. And like their American counterparts, they are increasingly focused on metrics of success and looking toward philanthropic advisors to provide education about sectors or regions or due diligence on individual charities.

LGT Venture Philanthropy exemplifies the trend toward strategic philanthropy and the demand for advisory services in the region. LGT VP is the philanthropic arm of LGT Bank, the largest private bank in Liechtenstein, led by CEO Prince Max von Liechtenstein. Liechtenstein launched LGT VP as a vehicle for his own giving and it is now inviting other investors to contribute to its approved projects or contract for its due diligence and advisory services. LGT VP offers grant funding, as well as loans and investments and managerial guidance and strategy development.

In the two years since the organization was founded, it has provided funding for nine organizations. A typical recipient has been in operation for at least five years, and has a model that can be brought to scale. One organization to which LGT VP has provided investment capital is Husk Power Systems in Bihar, India. Bihar is a significant rice-growing area, and as a result produces tons of agricultural waste in the form of processed rice husks. HPS is using the resulting biomass to create fuel and provide electricity to rural villages presently dependent upon kerosene, a dirty and expensive alternative.[23]

For some donors in Europe, partnerships with other donors, including corporations or public institutions, are the key to achieving the greater impact promised by strategic philanthropy. In Tanzania, WISE, a philanthropy advisory company based in Switzerland, helped broker an alliance of three major individual donors and CAMFED (Campaign for Female Education), a charity focused on improving girls' access to education in Africa. The alliance will invest some $950,000 over five years to dramatically scale up CAMFED programs in six local districts.

Ana Feder of the European Foundation Center says she is seeing an increased trend of cooperation among organizations in Europe to address social problems.[24] For example, the Fundazioni4Africa, a joint venture among four Italian

European philanthropists, like their American counterparts, are increasingly focused on metrics of success and looking toward philanthropic advisors to provide education about sectors or regions or due diligence on individual charities.

bank-based foundations, is working in Northern Uganda to reintegrate people displaced by fighting by the Lord's Resistance Army. Fundazioni4Africa is also collaborating with a community of Senegalese immigrants living in Italy on a project to improve the living standards in Senegal's urban slums.

There is also growing interest in Europe in social investment funds. Social investment funds have emerged as alternative vehicles for investing in businesses that aim to earn profits while contributing to positive social outcomes. Steve Beck, general partner of SpringHill Ventures, a social private equity firm, says that Europe's lagging legal framework for philanthropy and non-profits actually has accelerated interest in social investing: "European pension funds led by the Dutch have embraced 'social' or 'impact' investing more readily than U.S. funds. One reason for this is that the line between the for-profit and non-profit sectors is not as bright or impermeable in Europe as it is in the U.S.," he says.[25]

Even traditional European charities like OxFam are creating social investment programs. OxFam's Enterprise Development Programme, while just a small part of the organization, utilizes loans alongside conventional grant-making. According to Malcolm Fleming of OxFam Scotland, the organization hopes this market-led approach will offer greater engagement and appeal to new philanthropists and other entrepreneurs.[26]

ASIAN PHILANTHROPY

Philanthropy in Asia has registered significant growth in the past few years, largely due to increased engagement by individuals in China and India. A report conducted during 2008 by the UK-based Charities Aid Foundation shows that 41% of Indians and 80% of Chinese gave money to charitable causes during that year.[27] Another report prepared for Give2Asia's Beijing Philanthropy Forum showed that in the years leading up to 2008, charitable donations in China had sustained annual growth above 65%.[28] In 2008 giving increased to three times that level as a result of the humanitarian response to the Sichuan earthquake that killed 70,000 people and left five million homeless. Dien Yuen, Director of Philanthropy at Give2Asia, wrote recently that the humanitarian reaction to the earthquake "fast forwarded China's charitable sector development and activated ideas of how and what Chinese philanthropy could become."[29]

The philanthropic environments of donor countries such as Australia, New Zealand and Japan are significantly ahead of China and India. The Charities Aid Foundation in Australia reports that the amount given by individual donors has increased by about 88% since 1997—12.5% on average per year.[30] On the other hand, New Zealand's $1.2 billion philanthropic sector receives proportionately few funds from private individuals. Only 20% of nonprofit funding comes from direct individual donations.[31]

Ninety percent of Japanese individuals give, with an average donation of about $30 per household per year.[32] Most of those donations go to community organizations. There are only about 1,000 organizations in Japan that enjoy tax exempt nonprofit status, a consequence of Japanese policy that makes it difficult to achieve nonprofit status and difficult to keep it. It is also culturally prohibited to solicit donations from the public. As a result, individual philanthropy represents a very small percentage of society's engagement in social issues.[33]

CONCLUSION

Overall, the most important trends in international philanthropy outside of the United States are growth and dynamism. What have traditionally been very different philanthropic cultures are increasingly converging. But rather than bringing homogeneity, this convergence is bringing more innovation in the philanthropic sector. A good example is the emergence of social stock exchanges in Brazil and South Africa. These exchanges work much like traditional for-profit capital markets to facilitate the flow of philanthropic capital, demonstrating that innovation in philanthropy is now being imported to as well as exported from the United States.

Growing Enterprise from the Ground Up

SHELL FOUNDATION

What if a company realizes that "business as usual" is no longer an option? That's what energy giant Shell discovered in the mid-1990s after a series of environmental and human rights controversies left it questioning the way it did business. A survey of opinion makers, journalists, advocacy groups, members of the public and its own executives convinced the company that it needed to incorporate the principles of sustainable development into its business model. In 1997, Shell decided that it would launch a global, social investment effort that culminated in the creation of the Shell Foundation in 2000 as an independent charity registered in the United Kingdom.

The foundation's mission is to develop, scale-up and promote enterprise-based solutions to development challenges related to poverty and the environment, focusing on projects that jointly engaged business and society. The foundation, which had assets of about $409 million in 2007, spends approximately $16 million each year, leveraging several times that from strategic partners and investors. One of the foundation's core programs is Aspire, which focuses on helping small and medium-sized enterprises (SME's) in Africa fulfill their potential through business development assistance and risk capital.

Through a close partnership with GroFin, a specialist SME financier, Shell Foundation helped pioneer a new business model specifically designed to plug the "missing middle"—financing for start-ups that are too large to qualify for microfinance loans but too small to get funding from banks or other traditional sources of capital. Having grown from two employees in 2003 to a specialized finance company with 100 employees in eight countries, GroFin is at the forefront of efforts to provide risk finance to SMEs in Africa. It has $250 million under its management invested by organizations such as the International Finance Corporation, the European Investment Bank, and the African Development Bank. It is funding 151 businesses and has created and is sustaining 5,686 jobs. In a testament to its work in this sector, GroFin has been an Africa Investor Award winner every year since 2005.

> Shell Foundation helped pioneer a new business model specifically designed to plug the "missing middle" —financing for start-ups that are too large to qualify for microfinance loans but too small to get funding from banks or other sources.

Chris West, the director of the Shell Foundation, is proud of GroFin's development, but says it has not been easy. "We've only managed to get where we are with a phenomenal amount of effort," he says, noting that it takes a huge commitment to make an organization like GroFin financially viable. To date, the Shell Foundation has invested about $20 million in GroFin as a mixture of development assistance and risk capital. It also holds a $15 million equity stake in the GroFin Africa Fund.

West stresses, however, that the relationship is more than financial. "It's genuinely a partnership," he says, noting that what distinguishes the Shell Foundation from other investors in GroFin is the amount of support the foundation provides in terms of marketing the GroFin model and raising investment capital.

"We're trying to promote the idea of 'growth finance,'" said West, assisting those businesses in the developing world with the greatest potential for rapid expansion. While these businesses have the potential for profitability, West stresses that this is not the main attraction for the Shell Foundation. "The financial return is a means to an end, where the end is to convince other big investors to invest in this space," he notes.

Luba Schotter is a small entrepreneur in South Africa whose business has grown with the help of GroFin. Having been turned down by commercial lending institutions, she turned to GroFin for a loan and business development assistance. With its help, she was able to grow Allday EnerGi Foods, which manufactures healthy and convenient low Glycemic Index foods, expanding the plant to three times its original size and hiring 15 new employees. Production has been streamlined and the business is set to grow further.

West is convinced that the SME sector will be at the forefront of efforts to develop African economies. And though GroFin is making inroads into this area, "$250 million is just a pin-prick compared to what SMEs in Africa need," he notes. However, having illustrated that this model is viable, he hopes that other investors will be drawn to the field. —**Eimear O'Leary-Barrett**

Glamour for a Cause

M·A·C AIDS FUND

When Frank Toskan and the late Frank Angelo, founders of the widely popular M·A·C make-up line, were considering a philanthropic direction for the Canadian company, they wanted to incorporate their employees' wishes in the decision and respond to the profound sense of loss in the fashion industry caused by the AIDS epidemic. It was fitting then that the decision to target HIV/AIDS was made by an employee vote in 1994 and the M·A·C Aids Fund was born. To date, the M·A·C Aids Fund has raised $180 million for HIV/AIDS-related causes through the sale of M·A·C's VIVA GLAM lipstick and lipglass. This makes M·A·C, which was acquired by the Estée Lauder company in 1998, the largest corporate, non-pharmaceutical contributor to the cause, according to Nancy Mahon, executive director of the M·A·C AIDS Fund.

Under the M·A·C VIVA Glam 100% Giving Model, 100% of the celebrity promoted sales of VIVA GLAM lipstick and lipglass go directly to the fund. This year's celebrity spokespersons are Lady Gaga and Cyndi Lauper. "We use famous spokesmodels because kids can identify with them and listen to them," said Mahon. The combination of glamorous celebrities and the fund's transparent giving model is highly appealing to customers, she noted. "It's a sort of guilt-free shopping," Mahon says.

The M·A·C AIDS Fund is a privately run foundation that puts a premium on making sure funding goes directly to programs and services. "Our operating cost is 7%, which is well-below the 10% golden standard within the industry," notes Mahon. About 65% of the program's funds are raised in the United States and 35% internationally; about 40% of the funds are channeled internationally and the rest are spent domestically in the United States.

In the developing world, the fund works in sub-Saharan Africa and the Caribbean, taking pride in an agile funding approach that seeks out underserved areas and moves rapidly to fill the need. "There is never enough money," says Mahon, "but there's plenty of good work to be done and we really refine our role and efforts on the HIV/AIDS cause."

In 2009, the fund launched the VIVA GLAM Global Partnership with an initial commitment of $2.5 million to collaborate with UNICEF and Nurturing Orphans for AIDS Humanity (NOAH) program. The funding expanded HIV testing for pregnant women in five South African provinces hard-hit by AIDS, allowing an additional 50,000 pregnant women to be tested for AIDS in 2009 and resulting in 12,000 HIV-positive mothers receiving treatment to prevent the transmission of HIV to their babies. The program has been expanded to test 100,000 women in 2010 and provide 28,000 courses of HIV-preventive medicine to pregnant

M·A·C Aids Fund VIVA Glam celebrity spokespersons Lady Gaga and Cyndi Lauper promote two new shades of VIVA GLAM lipstick. 100% of the sales of the lipstick go to the fund for HIV/AIDS prevention and treatment programs around the world.

women. The program is also expanding access to antiretroviral treatment for HIV-positive women and children and funding NOAH to provide food, shelter, and other basic necessities for 5,000 AIDS orphans in South Africa.

As part of the partnership, M·A·C has created an employee holiday drive in the United States and the United Kingdom to raise funds for school uniforms, school supplies, educational materials, and school fees for the children of NOAH. M·A·C employees are heavily invested in the M·A·C AIDS Fund, notes Mahon. "We have the best retention rate in the whole industry. This is because M·A·C as a company is clear to her values and commitment to conduct our business responsibly," she says.

—Ai Ghee Ong

INTERNATIONAL PVO

The Hope of the Land

Speranta Terrei

Hope does not come often for tuberculosis patients in low-income countries, who lack access to the care and counseling that can make the difference between the success and failure of TB treatment. But for TB patients in the tiny former Soviet republic of Moldova, hope makes house calls. Speranta Terrei, a Moldovan grassroots organization whose name translates to "Hope of the Land," brings treatment and patient education to the doorsteps of some of Moldova's most vulnerable people.

Founded in 2006, Speranta Terrei has two main purposes: promoting awareness of TB and assisting TB patients with treatment completion, an often daunting task for individuals burdened with poverty or substance abuse. People who do not complete the full course of treatment for TB are at risk of developing strains of TB that are resistant to the drugs commonly used to treat the disease. There are nearly 500,000 cases of multidrug-resistant TB, which is now recognized as a growing public health threat around the world.

Speranta Terrei, which is based in the northern Moldovan city of Balti, sends volunteer "moderators" to the homes of TB patients with the day's medication to make sure they are taking it on schedule. The moderators also answer questions about the disease and offer reassurance to patients throughout the treatment process. These volunteers, who are often people who have been cured of TB themselves, are meeting a critical need in Moldova, where 5,000 TB cases are detected annually and multidrug-resistant strains are widespread. TB patients tend to be from marginalized populations of low-income people, many of whom have AIDS or substance abuse problems. They may have difficulty getting to the dispensary to pick up their medication or are not convinced that TB is a treatable disease, making compliance with the necessary treatment regime difficult.

The personal relationships that develop between moderators and patients often contribute to successful treatment. For instance, Igor Zaporojan's diagnosis of TB and HIV left him and his mother, Galina, defeated and despondent. When moderator Serghei Tinica arrived at their doorstep, he was given a skeptical reception. Tinica persisted, however, visiting regularly and bringing TB drugs and a vivacious attitude. He explained the drug regimen and shared his own personal failings and triumphs with TB treatment. The personal attention paid off and Igor stuck with the treatment program—soon he gained weight and his eyes lost their hollowness. When he was cured of TB, both Igor and his mother enlisted in Speranta Terrei's training program as moderators, beginning their own journey through the streets of Balti to share their newfound hope.

In addition to treatment and counseling for TB patients, Speranta Terrei runs public awareness campaigns that reach some 17,500 Moldovans each year with educational messages

Galina, a volunteer moderator from Speranta Terrei, assists a patient in his recovery from tuberculosis in the former Soviet republic of Moldova. Moderators educate patients about TB and ensure they complete their treatment.

on recognizing TB symptoms and preventing transmission. For its dedicated and innovative efforts, Speranta Terrei was honored as the first recipient of the Tuberculosis Survival Prize in October 2008. This is a new annual award supported by a grant from Eli Lilly and Company and the Lilly MDR-TB Partnership to enable organizations that may have difficulty accessing funding to replicate or upscale their anti-TB efforts.

The $2,000 prize helped Speranta Terrei to pay for moderators' allowances, which are about $50 per month, and the production and broadcast of television and radio messages on tuberculosis. The award also generated invaluable publicity for the cause of TB treatment support. "The Tuberculosis Survival Prize brought attention to how few patients abandoned TB treatment under the supervision of moderators," said Feodora Rodiucova, Speranta Terrei's president.

Speranta Terrei plans to continue to bring hope to a land much in need of it and to play its part in the battle against TB.

—**Jason M. Farrell**

INTERNATIONAL PVO

What A Difference a House Makes

Niall Mellon Township Trust

Sophia Morris lived in a shack near Cape Town for 14 years. She and her family had no running water, no bath or shower, and no indoor toilet. Then in 2004, her meager shack burned down in a raging fire, pushing her already precarious existence into further disarray. But what could have been a tragedy turned into a stroke of good fortune because of the Niall Mellon Township Trust. In 2005, Irish volunteers with the Trust built Morris a brick house. For the first time in her life, she had running water, indoor plumbing and a real place to call home.

"Getting a brick house changed my whole life. I knew my children would be safe; we have a water heater for hot water, and you can sleep at night even if there is wind because it is not so loud, and we have no problems with rain," she said. Having a home has also helped Morris become economically self-sufficient because it allowed her to open a day care business. And it has made a huge difference in the life and future

"Getting a brick house changed my whole life. I knew my children would be safe; we have a water heater for hot water, and you can sleep at night even if there is wind because it is not so loud, and we have no problems with rain."

prospects of her children. "The house makes a big difference in the children's lives, as there is a stigma attached when you come from an informal settlement. People think you might be violent or a criminal," she said, adding, "So when you have a house everything is different!"

Founded in 2002 by Irish philanthropist and property developer Niall Mellon, who was startled by the horrendous living conditions he found in South African townships, the Niall Mellon Township Trust builds quality homes for impoverished communities of South Africa. According to Siomha Cunniffe, development coordinator for the Trust, before the arrival of the Trust, most residents of the townships lived in small, corrugated iron shacks measuring about nine feet by nine feet. Few had running water in their homes and most shared outdoor sanitation facilities. In 2002, the Trust built 150 homes. Since then, a total of 11,000 homes have been built—5,000 in 2008 alone.

The Trust operates on a partnership model. Each year it brings volunteers from around the world to participate in a week-long "building blitz." In 2008, 2,000 volunteers travelled from 13 countries to take part in a building blitz, constructing 253 homes. The Trust also builds homes year-round in partnership with local communities. Through the People's Housing Process (PHP), a service of the South African government that provides housing subsidies to the poor, communities work with the Trust on the planning and designing of communities. Local communities are involved with the building process as well. Most homes are built by local contract workers, of which the Trust employs approximately 2,000. It provides training in skills such as masonry, carpentry, painting, plumbing, and plastering. The Trust has a full-time staff of about 80 in South Africa that conducts the year-round building operation with some assistance from the headquarters in Ireland.

The Trust receives funding from the Irish government, the South African government, and private donations. In 2008, Niall Mellon received about $4 million from the Irish government, and a subsidy from the South African government of approximately $646 per house built. "The South African government provides a subsidy for each house and the Trust fundraises to 'top-up' the subsidy," Cunniffe said. "This way, the charity is able to build bigger, better-finished, and more environmentally friendly homes with features such as solar water heating and basic water conservation measures."

In addition to residential properties, the Trust has built community facilities such as community halls, libraries and communal gardens as part of a greater goal of community development. A study by Impact Consulting showed that the Trust has increased the quality of life for residents of South Africa with respect to health, employment, education, and safety, proving that development really does happen from the ground up.

—Zenah Hasan

A Baby Called "Hygeia"

The Health Insurance Fund

When Attahiru Aishetu found herself in labor and facing an emergency caesarean section, paying for the operation was the last thing she wanted to worry about. Thanks to the Hygeia Community Health Plan, part of a groundbreaking effort to introduce private health insurance to poor communities in Nigeria, she didn't have to. Instead of going into debt to pay for the procedure out-of-pocket, as many people in Nigeria do when faced with an unexpected health crisis, all of Aishetu's costs were paid by Hygeia, which is appropriately named after the Greek goddess of health. In fact, Aishetu's neighbors were so impressed when they found out that the Hygeia covered her operation that they started calling her new baby boy "Hygeia."

The Hygeia Community Health Plan is a project of the Health Insurance Fund, a foundation that provides subsidized private health insurance to low-income groups in sub-Saharan Africa. The Health Insurance Fund (HIF) was established in 2005 by Kees Storm, former CEO of AEGON, the global insurance company, and the PharmAccess Foundation, a Dutch nonprofit that pioneers private-sector healthcare solutions in Africa.

The Health Access Foundation has received initial support from a number of sources. In October 2006, the Dutch Minister of Development Cooperation provided a $147 million grant to HIF to develop and implement insurance plans in four African countries over six years. In 2008, the World Bank became a donor to HIF, and the governor of Kwara State in Nigeria contracted with HIF to co-fund the premiums of 71,000 low income workers in the Afon district.

The first HIF-backed plan, the Hygeia Community Health Plan, was launched in Nigeria in early 2007 to cover 115,000 previously uninsured individuals in a country that relies on a piecemeal system of low-quality public health care and expensive out-of-pocket private care. The plan was launched under the umbrella of Hygeia Nigeria Limited, which runs the popular Hygeia HMO in Nigeria, a non-subsidized health insurance product. The Hygeia Community Health Plan targets market women and their families in Lagos and farmers and their families in the rural Shonga community in Kwara State. Premiums are subsidized by HIF to encourage enrollment in

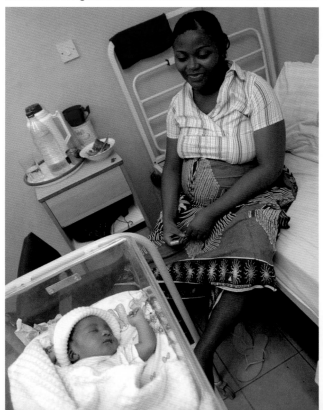

A member of the Hygeia Community Health Plan and her new baby. Thanks to this groundbreaking effort to introduce private health insurance to poor communities in Nigeria, 60,000 individuals now have affordable health care.

> Boupha may have spent the rest of her life homeless, picking garbage in the slums of Phnom Penh, but instead she found her way to shelter and vocational training run by Hagar International, which rehabilitates trafficking victims.

and improving standards. Overall, the clinics have improved significantly since the start of the program.

Currently 20,000 market women in Lagos and 40,000 farmers in Kwara State have access to quality basic healthcare, including HIV/AIDS treatment, through the Hygeia plan. Insurance programs for Tanzania and two other countries are being prepared to cover at least 230,000 previously uninsured low-income people.

—Zivile Gedrimaite

the plan. Premiums in the Lagos plan are $30 to $60 per year; members pay 8 to 15 percent of the premium in the first year. Enrollment in the plan is done on the spot by outreach workers with laptop computers.

Upgrading local health facilities to meet modern medical standards is a key part of the expansion of health care services. Hygeia is working with local facilities to upgrade 13 of the 19 clinics and hospitals (13 private and 6 public) contracted to provide care under the plan and Kwara State is paying to upgrade two of its public facilities.

According to Emma Coles, director of HIF, the goals of these initial plans are to build local administrative and medical capacity; to demonstrate that a market exists in Africa for private health insurance; and to increase investment in the health sector by leveraging public money to attract private funds. "The fund functions as a supply-and-demand based system in the private sector. This fund will enable low-income groups to receive collective health insurance through a premium subsidy. In addition, the care providers will be paid based on their performance, which will improve the quality of care," she said.

To date, these market factors appear to be working to improve the quality of health care in Nigeria. Clinics in the areas covered by the plan have seen a dramatic increase in patients. Kwara State Governor Dr. Bukola Saraki, chair of the Nigerian Governors' Association, has called the Hygeia plan "the best model" to address the issue of healthcare in Nigeria and in all of Africa."

HIF performs research to measure the impact of the program and provides quality control, making recommendations for improving current and future programs in terms of product design, targeting, and implementation. A PharmAccess team conducts two monitoring and evaluation visits a year to monitor the standards of care at clinics and hospitals in the program and to evaluate whether they are maintaining

Abandoned No More

HAGAR INTERNATIONAL

Poverty is abundant and hope is scarce in Cambodia. Some 77 percent of the population lives on less than $2 a day. With little economic opportunity, desperate Cambodians are easy prey for human traffickers. When 17-year-old Boupha was offered a job as a waitress in Phnom Penh for $50 a week, she quickly accepted, figuring that anything was better than eking out a living in the slums on the edge of the city. Instead of a waitressing job, however, she found herself sold to a brothel in the coastal town of Sihanoukville in southern Cambodia. Sexual exploitation became a way of life. "I wanted to run away but could not get out of the house. I felt like I wanted to end my life," she says.

Eventually Boupha escaped, but her stepmother was forced to sell their house to raise the $700 the brothel owner demanded for her freedom. Boupha may have spent the rest of her life homeless, picking garbage in the slums of Phnom Penh, but instead she found her way to shelter and vocational training run by Hagar International, a Switzerland-based Christian PVO. Hagar rehabilitates women and children who are victims of trafficking and domestic abuse. Now, at age 21, Boupha runs a beauty salon in her neighborhood. "Everybody in the village is very proud of me, I have done this all by myself. Because I have a good job, and have been able to open my own business, I have much more confidence," she said.

Hagar International was founded by Pierre and Simonetta Tami, who left their careers in Switzerland in 1991 to follow a spiritual mission in Cambodia. While in Cambodia, Pierre met a woman on her deathbed who changed the course of his life: "She talked, her tears running down her cheek trying to summarize

Women working at Hagar Catering, a full-service catering firm staffed by former trafficking victims that helps support Hagar's programs to rehabilitate women and children who have been trafficked.

her life full of destitution, harshness, brutality, lack of even the most basic of needs." The woman asked Pierre to promise that her children would not suffer the same fate. From this promise, Hagar was born, named in honor of the biblical Hagar who was cast into the desert with her child and rescued by God.

The Tami's opened a shelter for exploited and abandoned women and children in Phnom Penh in 1994 that became the basis for Hagar Cambodia, the mainstay of Hagar's operations. Hagar employs a social enterprise model that leverages economic empowerment to socially rehabilitate exploited women. "Doing one without the other is a great injustice to the very people we were seeking to empower. Having a job helps them to gain a positive outlook for the future and be successfully reintegrated into society," says Tami.

Hagar Cambodia's programs include shelters and trauma recovery centers to provide immediate housing and counseling to women and children who have been abused, abandoned or trafficked; education for children; literacy classes and vocational training for adults; and job placement. Its largest social enterprise is Hagar Catering, which began in 1998 as a small food cart franchise and is now a full-service catering and facilities management company that had $1.2 million in revenue in 2008 and includes the U.S. Embassy among its clients. In 2008, Hagar employed 466 people in its three social enterprises in Cambodia, which in addition to Hagar Catering include apparel and soy milk manufacturing businesses.

In addition to Hagar Cambodia, Hagar International has fundraising arms in the United States, Australia, New Zealand and Singapore. Hagar received just under $2.7 million in funding in 2008. Hagar receives about 70 percent of its funding from grants from foundations and NGOs, about 20 percent from individual donors, and the remainder from government donors and sales of products from its various enterprises.

Hagar's approach has proven highly effective in Cambodia; 80 percent of the women and children taken in are successfully reintegrated into society. It is only one of 10 nonprofits in the country to receive the "Good Practice Project" certification. Hagar is in the processing of replicating its work and holistic rehabilitation model in Afghanistan and Vietnam and is planning to expand into India.

In 2004, the U.S. State Department honored Pierre Tami as one of six "Heroes Acting To End Modern Day Slavery and Trafficking," but Tami says there is still much work to be done until trafficking is history.

—Emily Gikow

INDIGENOUS PHILANTHROPY SPOTLIGHT

Getting Down to Business in Latin America

FUNDES

Twenty-five years ago the unlikely combination of a Swiss businessman and the Archbishop of Panama surveyed the development landscape in Latin America and decided that micro, small and medium-sized enterprises (MSMEs) were key to social and economic growth in the region. It was a prescient insight, as MSMEs are now a cornerstone of economic development efforts in emerging economies around the world. The organization started by Stephan Schmidheiny and Archbishop Marcos McGrath of Panama, the Foundation for Sustainable Development (FUNDES), has been promoting the competitive development of MSMEs in Latin America since 1984.

Schmidheiny and Archbishop McGrath proved prescient, not just about the need for FUNDES but about the importance of MSMEs to Latin America. Today there are more than 18.5 million MSMEs in the region, providing 61.49 million jobs and contributing approximately 50 percent to Latin America's GDP.

"While credit access is critical, that's not the most important element for micro, small and medium-sized enterprises," according to FUNDES Executive Director Ulrich Frei. "Access to knowledge is more important to close the gap."

FUNDES started as a mico-credit provider, but learned that "while credit access is critical, that's not the most important element for MSMEs," says Executive Director Ulrich Frei, adding, "Access to knowledge is more important to close the gap."

FUNDES therefore changed its focus to business development training. With propriety methodologies that it created, FUNDES began to train small businesses on a one-to-one basis, providing knowledge transfer and consultancy. Their comprehensive consulting services help MSMEs respond to changing market environments and reinvent their interactions with business partners and stakeholders to learn to be competitive. "Our objective is for MSMEs to grow, and be more competitive and sustainable, as well as able to generate more wealth, employment, and well being," says Frei.

One such project occurred in Mexico, where local mom-and-pop stores were facing new competition from large retail chains. The local Ministry of the Economy wanted FUNDES to help these businesses develop new business models, diversify their services, and carve new niches for themselves. FUNDES developed a program targeted to the small retailers, training them to create and implement a new business model and working with them on point-of-sale marketing, stock management, business records, customer service, and energy conservation. FUNDES also guided the businesses to make infrastructure improvements, including modernizing stores, and helped them obtain financing to purchase new equipment. As a result, sales for these mom-and-pop stores increased by 32 percent and their number of clients increased by 47 percent. The local government estimates that 2,432 local jobs were maintained and 152 new jobs were created.

A local business owner expressed his gratitude for the training that has allowed his store to prosper. "Thanks to the benefits that the program has given us, my children are doing what they want. They are studying, they are attending the university and this is what is most important to me," said Martín Miranda Silva. This program was so successful that the federal Mexican Government has extended it throughout the country.

Since it began offering training and consulting services, FUNDES has developed 159 training modules and has trained some 320,000 program participants. As of 2009, FUNDES is operating in 10 countries throughout Latin America: Argentina, Bolivia, Chile, Colombia, Costa Rica, El Salvador, Guatemala, Mexico, Panama, and Venezuela. FUNDES is largely self-sustaining; 80 percent of its financing comes from the provision of consulting services, while the rest comes from partnerships with local and national governments, corporations, and multilateral organizations. Despite its success, FUNDES remains true to the vision of its founders, constantly striving to create a nimble organization willing to take risks to promote private-sector growth in Latin America.

—Ai Ghee Ong

INDIGENOUS PHILANTHROPY SPOTLIGHT

Changing the Fate of Slum Children

PARIKRMA HUMANITY FOUNDATION

It seemed that Chandru Ramesh's fate was sealed. Born in the teeming slums of Bangalore, India, so memorably revealed to the world in the film "Slumdog Millionaire" with an unemployed, alcoholic father, he appeared destined to remain uneducated and in poverty. But the Parikrma Humanity Foundation has rewritten the future for Ramesh and hundreds of children like him in India's slums. Through the foundation, Ramesh is now enrolled in a Parikrma school, getting the education that will allow him to escape poverty. The seven-year-old loves math and English and hopes one day to be a police officer.

The Parikrma Humanity Foundation is a nonprofit organization dedicated to breaking the cycle of poverty in urban India by providing free, top-notch education to otherwise uneducated children. The foundation was founded in 2003 by Shukla Bose, the former managing director of Resort Condominiums International and India's Woman Entrepreneur of the Year in 1995. Bose left behind nearly 30 years in the corporate world to plunge into India's growing philanthropy sector. "I was good at making profit-

Born in the teeming slums of Bangalore, India, so memorably revealed to the world in the film "Slumdog Millionaire" with an unemployed, alcoholic father, Chandru Ramesh appeared destined to remain uneducated and in poverty.

able businesses, but there was something telling me that I wasn't using my full potential. Rather than making healthy balance sheets, I wanted to do more," Bose said of her career change.

Having volunteered with Mother Teresa, Bose knew what kind of work and dedication was needed for social change at the grassroots level and knew exactly where she wanted to start—with the substandard schools of India's urban slums, where instruction is haphazard, teacher standards are nonexistent and attendance is as low as 15 percent. "I was very conscious of the inequities that existed...I knew for sure that education was the only way people from marginalized sections of society could cross that border," she said.

Parikrma employs a 360° Development Program that it developed to ensure the greatest possible benefit to poor students. The program includes English instruction from well-trained teachers; three meals daily to ensure that at least

80 percent of children's calorie requirements are met; health care, including immunizations, and a cadre of social workers who work with parents and the community to create nurturing home environments.

Parikrma serves orphaned or abandoned children and those in homes with incomes below RS 1500 ($30) per month. The organization places special emphasis on educating girls, with the goal of increasing female empowerment. In addition to free education and meals for the children, Parikrma offers free community development programs, such as addiction recovery and microcredit programs.

Bose funded the organization with her own assets for its first eight months of operation, but knew her resources wouldn't last forever so she contacted her former corporate network. "I was very clear that I didn't want to ask people for funds until I had something to show. I started talking to all my past business associates and telling them the story of what we're doing," Bose said. Today, the foundation is funded by Indian corporations such as TNT India Private Limited and ING Vysya Bank, as well as multi-national and U.S. corporations with operations in India, such as Levi Strauss, Adobe, AT&T and Dell.

There are currently 1,115 children in the four Parikrma schools in Bangalore, with plans to expand. The foundation wants to serve as a model for other organizations interested in starting schools for the poor and scale-up its model through partnerships. Early results of the model are promising. A 2007 Nielsen Co. study commissioned by Parikrma found that academically, children in the Parikrma schools are performing far better than children from government schools and are on par with children from private schools. The study also found that children in the Parikrma schools are more confident and have better self-esteem than children in government or private schools. The vast majority of Parikrma students were able to name their professional goals for the future and had confidence that they would reach them—no small achievement for children from the slums. Bose is confident that the Parikrma model will help more and more children achieve their potential, no matter where they were born. — Zenah Hasan

Children play at a school in India funded by the Parikrma Humanity Foundation. The foundation is providing a free, high-quality education to some 1,100 children from the Bangalore slums.

1 Organisation for Economic Co-Operation and Development, *OECD Journal on Development: Development Co-operation Report 2009*, Table 13.

2 Ibid.

3 Ibid.

4 Ibid.

5 Ibid.

6 Ibid.

7 Ibid.

8 Ibid.

9 Ibid.

10 Ibid.

11 European Foundation Centre, "Foundations in the European Union," May 2008, http://www.efc.be/NewsKnowledge/Documents/EFC-RTF_EU%20Foundations-Facts%20and%20Figures_2008.pdf (accessed Feb. 3, 2010).

12 Ibid.

13 Bertelsmann Stiftung, "Stiftungen en Deutschland–Die wichtigsten Fakten und Zahlen," http://www.bertelsmann-stiftung.de/cps/rde/xbcr/SID-2C6C0B25-476BEBE6/bst_engl/Stiftungen_in_Deutschland_factsheet_0209.pdf (accessed November 2, 2009).

14 Philanthropy UK, 2009, "Top 10 Trends in British Philanthropy," http://www.philanthropyuk.org/Resources/Top10trends (accessed November 2, 2009).

15 This is a consensus view of various experts consulted, including Caroline Hartnell, Editor, *Alliance* Magazine, telephone interview, September 14, 2009; Etienne Eichenberger, Executive Director, WISE (wise investor/social

entrepreneur), telephone interview October 19, 2009; and Judith Symonds, Principal, JCS International Philanthropy & Strategy Advisors, telephone interview, October 30, 2009.

16 Telephone interview with Wolfgang Hafenmeyer, October 12, 2009.

17 Caroline Hartnell, "Highlights of the Symposium," *Alliance* Magazine Special Supplement: European Foundations in Times of Crisis, http://www.alliancemagazine.org/members/pdfs/bdl-supplement.pdf (Feb. 2, 2010).

18 Telephone Interview with Judith Symonds, Principal, JCS International Philanthropy & Strategy Advisors, October 30, 2009.

19 Ibid.

20 Banque de Luxembourg, "Philanthropy Increases despite the Recession," http://www.philanthropie.lu/fr/entry/philanthropy-increases-despite-the-recession (accessed November 2, 2009).

21 Telephone interview with Michael Alberg-Seberich, October 20, 2009.

22 "Views from the Advisors," *Alliance* Magazine Special Supplement: European Foundations in Times of Crisis, http://www.alliancemagazine.org/members/pdfs/bdlsupplement.pdf (Feb. 2, 2010).

23 Husk Power Systems, http://www.huskpowersystems.com/Home.htm, retrieved November 2, 2009.

24 Telephone interview with Ana Feder, November 2, 2009.

25 Telephone interview with Steve Beck, October 31, 2009.

26 "Is Philanthropy 'Just Giving'?" European Association for Philanthropy and Giving Roundtable, Oct. 13, 2009.

27 Charities Aid Foundation, "Giving to Charities Widespread in BRIC Countries," http://www.cafonline.org/default.aspx?page=16781 (accessed November 2, 2009). The report authors believe the Chinese numbers are elevated due to increased engagement in 2008 as a result of the Sichuan earthquake that occurred in May of that year.

28 Dien Yuen, 2009, "Philanthropy during the Sichuan Earthquake," http://tacticalphilanthropy.com/2009/10/philanthropy-in-china-part-ii (accessed November 2, 2009).

29 Ibid.

30 CAF Australia, "Financial Downturn hits Charity Donors" July 2 2009, http://www.cafaustralia.org.au/media_releases.php (accessed November 3, 2009).

31 D. Robinson and Pat Hanley "Funding New Zealand 2002: Resource flows to the community non-profit sector in New Zealand," Social and Civic Policy Institute, http://giving.org.nz/files/Funding%20NZ%202002.pdf (accessed October 19, 2009).

32 Ian Wilhelm, "Japanese Charities Urged to do more to Help Charities," *The Chronicle of Philanthropy*, (accessed November 2, 2009).

33 Japan Center for International Exchange, "New Tax Bill Gives Partial Victory to NPOs," *Civil Society Monitor* No. 6, July 2002, http://www.jcie.or.jp/civilnet/monitor/6.html (accessed October 19, 2009).

SIDEBAR, PAGE 44

1 Jim O'Neill, "Building Better Global Economic BRICS," Goldman Sachs Global Economic Paper No. 66, Nov. 30, 2001.

2 Andrew Kramer, "Emerging Economies Meet in Russia," *The New York Times*, June 16, 2009.

3 Candace Lessa and Fernando Rossetti, "The Future of Philanthropy in Brazil: Creating a more Diverse Sector," Synergos Knowledge Resources, 2005.

4 Margarida Pfeifer, "The new philanthropy: Latin America Inc. turns to foundations as a strategy for serving social ends," *Latin Trade*, January 2007.

5 Candace Lessa and Fernando Rossetti, "The Future of Philanthropy in Brazil: Creating a more Diverse Sector," Synergos Knowledge Resources, 2005.

6 "Case studies of organizations supporting community foundations," Institute for the Development of Social Investment, http://www.wingsweb.org/download/csv2_idis.pdf (accessed Oct. 20, 2009).

7 Olga Alexeeva, "Russia: Historic Growth in Individual Giving," *Philanthropy UK Newsletter*, http://www.philanthropyuk.org/Newsletter/Sep2008Issue34/Russia (accessed Oct. 24, 2009).

8 Ibid.

9 Ibid.

10 Alexander Livshin and Richard Weitz, "Civil Society and Philanthropy Under Putin," *International Journal of Not-for-Profit Law*, Volume 8, Issue 3, May 2006.

11 Ibid.

12 Ibid.

13 Jamey Gambrell, "Philanthropy in Russia: New Money Under Pressure," *Carnegie Reporter* Vol. 3 No. 1, 2004.

14 Alexander Livshin and Richard Weitz, Civil Society and Philanthropy Under Putin, *International Journal of Not-for-Profit Law*, Volume 8, Issue 3, May 2006.

15 *Invisible but Widespread: The Nonprofit Sector in India*, PRIA, 2003.

16 Dr. Sandeep Deshmukh, "India: myriad shapes of philanthropy," *Philanthropy UK Newsletter*, http://www.philanthropyuk.org/Newsletter/Sep2008Issue34/India (accessed Oct. 30, 2009).

17 India's Tata Group: Empowering marginalized communities, *Global Giving Matters*, Feb/April 2005.

18 Dean Nelson, "Where Are India's Great Philanthropists," Telegraph.co.UK, http://blogs. telegraph.co.uk/news/deannelson/100004813/where-are-indias-great-philanthropists/(accessed Oct. 30, 2009).

19 Shantanu Guha Ray, "The Philanthropy Conundrum," *Tehelka Magazine*, Feb. 28, 2009.

20 Centre for Advancement of Philanthropy, http://www.karmayog.com/ngos/cap.htm (accessed Oct. 30, 2009).

21 Ariana Eunjung Cha, "China's Pusher of Philanthropy," *The Washington Post*, Jan. 31, 2009.

22 China: Policy Environment, Asia Pacific Philanthropy Consortium, http://www.asiapacificphilanthropy.org/profile-ch4 (accessed Nov. 4, 2009).

23 China Charity Donation Information Center, "2009 First-Half Year Report on Charitable Donations in China," October 2009.

24 "Jet Li One Foundation: 1 Yuan to Spread the Disease of Love," The Hauser Center for Nonprofit Organizations, http://hausercenter.org/chinanpo/2009/07/one-foundation-1-yuan-to-spread-the-disease-of-love/ (accessed Nov. 4, 2009).

25 Eunjung Cha, "China's Pusher of Philanthropy," *The Washington Post*, Jan. 31, 2009.

GLOBAL REMITTANCES

Providing Stability in an Economic Storm

Remittances remain one of the most important, but also least understood, private global capital flows. They are important both because they provide a lifeline for many poor families by facilitating the purchase of food, education, housing and medical care, and because they exceed Official Development Assistance (ODA) and private philanthropy to the developing world. They are little understood because research and practice into finding effective ways to harness this large flow for development purposes are still in their infancy.

As predicted in last year's *Index*, remittances to developing countries have remained a remarkably resilient economic flow during the global recession. Remittances to developing countries continued to rise in 2008, slowing only in the last

quarter. All remittances to developing countries totaled $338 billion in 2008, a 17% increase from 2007 and almost three times the total in 2002.[1] Because an unknown percentage of remittances flow through informal channels, the true total is likely larger. Remittances remain the dominant financial flow to developing nations, exceeding both ODA and philanthropy.

According to Dilip Ratha of the World Bank, remittances are predicted to fall to $317 billion in 2009, but this 6.1% decline is smaller than the earlier prediction of a 7.3% decrease. Remittance flows are expected to remain flat in 2010 and recover modestly in 2011, with a predicted growth rate of 4%. At the same time, they are expected to remain more resilient than other private capital flows, which will increase their importance to developing countries.[2] The regions expected to see the largest declines in 2009 are Europe and Central Asia (15%), followed by Latin America and the Caribbean (7%), and the Middle East and North Africa (6%).[3]

According to Ratha, there are a number of reasons for the relative resilience of remittances. Remittances are sent home by the total stock of migrants, and not just recent migrants, so they will continue to flow even after migration decreases as a result of a recession-induced drop in demand for employment. In addition, they tend to be a small portion of migrants' incomes. Migrants may economize in other ways, such as sharing housing, to be able to continue to send the same amount of money home. And the stimulus measures undertaken in many Western countries may be increasing demand in housing and other fields that are dependent on migrant labor, increasing employment for the many migrants.[4]

The Center for Global Prosperity was one of the first institutions to discuss the significance of remittances to development in publications dating back to 2002. We continue to document their magnitude and uses in poverty reduction. The development community at large is paying attention to these flows as well. The World Bank tracks remittance flows and publicizes their role in development and in 2009 held two conferences on the subject.[5] The International Fund for Agriculture Development's International Forum on Remittances, held in Africa in October 2009, brought together key players in remittances, migration, and finance.[6] The third annual Global Forum on Migration and Development, held in November 2009, focused on migration and remittances and how to engage the private sector on issues related to migration and development.[7]

While remittances are gaining ground as a policy issue, mechanisms to leverage these flows are still being perfected. Calling remittances the link between migration and development, Ratha has called for the creation of an international body, an International Remittances Institute, "that would monitor the flows of labor and remittances and oversee policies to make them easier, cheaper, safer, and more productive."[8] Such an institution has been proposed by the African Union and the European Union on a regional scale.

REMITTANCE FLOWS AND TRENDS

As noted, remittances from all countries to developing countries totaled $338 billion in 2008, compared to the revised total of $289 billion in 2007. There were important differences, however, in remittance growth by migration corridor. Remittance flows to South Asia increased 36% to $73 billion in 2008 despite the global recession, outpacing earlier predictions. Remittances to East Asia and the Pacific were also strong, increasing 21% in 2008 to $86 billion. In the Latin American and Caribbean region, however, which is largely dependent on the U.S. economy for employment, remittances grew by only 2% in 2008 to a total of $65 billion. The dramatic growth rate of remittances to sub-Saharan Africa halted, largely due to a drop in flows to Nigeria, for year-to-year growth of 13% in 2008 compared to 48% the previous year. Remittances to sub-Saharan Africa totaled $21 billion in 2008. Flows to Europe and Central Asia also slowed substantially to a 14% growth rate for a total of $58 billion, while remittance growth to the Middle East and North Africa was cut in half to 11% for a total of $35 billion.[9]

As in recent years, the largest receivers of remittances in 2008 were India, China, and Mexico. While India and China witnessed huge remittance increases in 2008, flows to Mexico remained relatively stable. Remittances to India grew from $37 billion in 2007 to $52 billion in 2008. Remit-

Remittances from all countries to developing countries totaled $338 billion in 2008, compared to $289 billion in 2007. The largest receivers of remittances were India, China and Mexico.

tances to China increased from $26 billion in 2007 to $49 billion in 2008.[10] Both India and China send a large number of migrants to Gulf Cooperation Council (GCC) countries such as Bahrain, Saudi Arabia and the United Arab Emirates, which have not felt the effects of the recession as much as other parts of the world.[11] Remittances to Mexico, however, remained basically stable, at $26 billion in 2008.[12]

Rounding out the top ten remittance receiving countries in 2008 were the Philippines, Poland, Nigeria, Romania, Bangladesh, Egypt and Vietnam. While larger nations such as China and India are top recipients of remittances in terms of gross amounts, remittances tend to account for a larger portion of GDP in smaller nations. As a fraction of national GDP, Tajikistan remains first, with remittances accounting for up 50% of its economy in 2008.[13] Other countries in which remittances account for more that 25% of GDP are Tonga, Moldova, Kyrgyzstan, and Lesotho.[14]

Latin America has been particularly hard hit by the decline in remittances. It was one of the first regions to feel the effects of the financial crisis, which hit earlier in the United States and Spain—the top migration destinations for Latin American immigrants— than in other countries. Remittances to this region began to slow in early 2008. The slow-down in the U.S. housing market, a major employment sector for Latin American immigrants, was largely to blame for the decline in remittances. While remittances to Latin American and Caribbean countries are predicted to continue their decline through 2009, a mild recovery is possible in 2010 or 2011 in tandem with the U.S. economy.[15]

There are factors that may constrain remittance growth over the next few years. The World Bank predicts that the weak job market will likely linger through 2011, resulting in less work for migrants abroad and lower levels of remittances. Also tighter immigration controls in both the United States and Europe, which depress migration, could perpetuate the slow recovery in remittance flows.[16] There is little evidence, however, that migrants are returning home. Most apparently have chosen to wait out the recession in their host country for fear that they will not be able to migrate in the future. It is also likely that observed remittance declines are an overestimate. Migrants may be sending remittances through cheaper, or even free, informal channels, such as sending money home with friends, which may make a larger portion of remittances untraceable.[17]

REMITTANCES FROM DONOR COUNTRIES TO THE DEVELOPING WORLD

In 2008, total remittances from the OECD's 22 Development Assistance Committee (DAC) members to the devel-

oping world are estimated to be $180.7 billion.[18] This is an increase of 15% percent from the updated 2007 figure of $157.0 billion. The total amount of remittances from DAC countries of $180.7 billion in 2008 was almost 50% more than total ODA of $121.5 billion for the same period. Of all remittances sent to developing countries, Asia received the greatest portion, with 43%. Latin America followed with 31%, the Middle East and North Africa received 11%, sub-Saharan Africa received 8%, and Europe and Central Asia received 7%.

U.S. remittances accounted for more than half, or $96.8 billion, of the total remittances sent to developing countries from the DAC donor countries. This is a 12% increase from the updated 2007 figure of $86.2 billion. Regionally, the main recipients of U.S. remittances were Latin American and the Caribbean, which received $46.8 billion, or 48%, followed by Asia and the Pacific, which received $39.2 billion, or 41%. Sub-Saharan Africa received $4.8 billion, or 5%, and $3.9 billion, or 4%, went to the Middle East. Europe and Central Asia received the least amount of remittances from the United States, amounting to $2 billion, or 2% of the total.

The single largest country recipient of U.S. remittances was Mexico, which received an estimated $24.2 billion in remittances from the United States in 2008, down nearly $1 billion from the updated 2007 figure of $25.1 billion. Mexico was followed by India, with $10.6 billion in remittances, an increase of just over $2 billion from the updated 2007 figure of $8.5 billion, and the Philippines, with $10.4 billion, a $1.3 billion increase from 2007.

Europe was the second-largest source of remittances to the developing world, with an estimated $58.5 billion sent from European donor countries, a 19% increase from the updated 2007 figure of $49.1 billion. The United Kingdom was the single largest source of remittances from Europe, at $13.6 billion, followed by Germany at $10.6 billion and France at $8.8 billion. The remaining DAC donor countries— Canada, Japan, Australia and New Zealand—accounted for $25.4 billion of remittances to the developing world. Canada accounted for the largest share of the remaining remittance

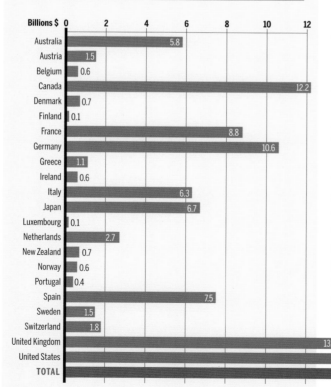

Figure 1

Remittances from OECD Donor Countries to Developing Countries, 2008 (Billions of $)

Country	Billions $
Australia	5.8
Austria	1.5
Belgium	0.6
Canada	12.2
Denmark	0.7
Finland	0.1
France	8.8
Germany	10.6
Greece	1.1
Ireland	0.6
Italy	6.3
Japan	6.7
Luxembourg	0.1
Netherlands	2.7
New Zealand	0.7
Norway	0.6
Portugal	0.4
Spain	7.5
Sweden	1.5
Switzerland	1.8
United Kingdom	13.6
United States	96.8
TOTAL	180.7

Source: Center for Global Prosperity calculations using World Bank data; see Methodology.

Diaspora Bonds

BY DILIP RATHA

With disaster recovery still underway in Haiti, diaspora bonds could be an important and innovative source of funding for long-term recovery.

Even as practitioners and policymakers are considering ways to leverage remittance flows to promote development, there are other existing, but underused, ways to leverage diasporas. Diaspora communities tend to remain loyal to their countries of origin and can serve as an important source of inexpensive and stable financing during harsh economic times. Some developing nation governments have issued diaspora bonds to tap into the assets of migrant communities living abroad. These bonds engage expatriates in the economic development of their home country by enabling patriotic investors to provide hard currency financing. Unlike foreign currency deposits, which can be cashed out at any moment, diaspora bonds are long-term deposits that are withdrawn once they reach maturity, making them a stable source of currency that can be used for investment.

Governments have issued these bonds at a "patriotic discount"— selling them at above-market prices to investors abroad who, as a result of their patriotism and their unique ability to deal with currency devaluation and other aspects of sovereign risk, are willing to pay such rates. This makes diaspora bonds an inexpensive way to raise funds.

Diaspora bonds have been in use since the 1950s, but few governments have actually enacted this innovative tool for financing. Countries such as Israel and India that have explored diaspora bonds have seen positive results. The Israeli government started issuing bonds in 1951 and is estimated to have raised $25 billion to date.

India first issued diaspora bonds during an economic crisis in 1991 when India experienced a large trade deficit, high inflation, devaluation of the Indian Rupee, and a large fiscal deficit. To quickly increase the foreign exchange reserves, the State Bank of India issued Indian Development Bonds that had a maturity term of five years and cost a minimum of $2,000. These bonds, which were directed specifically to members of the Indian diaspora, enabled India to raise $1.6 billion in a short period of time, which was critical to India's recovery from the crisis. India continued issuing bonds to its diaspora in 1998 and 2000, with returns ranging between 7% and 9%. To date, the Indian government has raised $11 billion through diaspora bonds.

Diaspora bonds are more likely to have success in countries that have a sizable, well-established, first generation diaspora, preferably in a high-income country. Additionally, in order for diaspora to invest in such bonds, the home country needs to have a minimum level of governance—countries with civil unrest are too risky for even the most patriotic investor. And while not absolutely necessary, having a banking network present in the host country linked to the diaspora can be helpful in advertising and selling these bonds.

Several countries, including Ethio-pia, Nepal, the Philippines, Rwanda, and Sri Lanka, are considering or have recently issued diaspora bonds to bridge financing gaps. Diaspora bonds also have been proposed for financing reconstruction in Haiti after the recent devastating earthquake. If 200,000 Haitians in the United States, Canada and France were to invest $1,000 each in diaspora bonds, it would add up to $200 million. In reality, much larger sums could be raised for Haiti through diaspora bonds. Given the high degree of political risk in the country, however, credit enhancement from creditworthy donors would be necessary. Preliminary calculation suggests that a $100 million grant from official or private donors to guarantee such bonds (say, for 10 years, on an annual rolling basis) could generate $600 million of funding for Haiti. Marketing diaspora bonds in the United States would require a temporary exemption from SEC regulations, but such bonds remain an innovative option for developing countries.

Dilip Ratha is the lead economist, Migration and Remittances Team, Development Prospects Group, at the World Bank. His research involves financing development in poor countries, including leveraging remittances and migration for development.

flows, at \$12.2 billion, followed by Japan at \$6.7 billion.

In terms of geographic trends in remittance flows from DAC donor countries, France is the largest source of remittances to the Middle East and North Africa, with \$5.9 billion in flows to this region, largely as a result of high flows to Morocco, Tunisia and Algeria. Germany is the largest source of remittances to Eastern Europe and Central Asia, contributing \$5 billion. The United Kingdom and the United States accounted for 62% of the flows to sub-Saharan Africa, with \$3.7 and \$4.8 billion, respectively.

REMITTANCES IN DEVELOPMENT

Research has linked remittances with poverty alleviation and increased expenditures on human capital. New research also suggests that remittances act as a form of insurance for households in countries susceptible to natural disasters or civil crisis. In Ethiopia, remittance receiving households use their cash reserves during times of food shocks, while non-receivers are more likely to sell valuable assets. Households receiving remittances in Burkina Faso and Ghana are more likely to have concrete houses as opposed to mud ones and have a greater access to communications, both of which help households overcome harsh conditions. In general, remittance flows increase during and after natural disasters and other crises, indicating that they are an important financial backstop.[19]

New research also shows that remittances can increase the long-term well being of households, and possibly communities, by fostering access to basic utilities. A study of remittance-receiving households in Mexico found that they had better access to modern water and sanitation facilities than non-receiving households. Remittances allowed these households to build the infrastructure to connect to existing municipal water systems and to install septic tanks for sewage disposal.[20]

The question of how to channel remittances to have a greater development impact remains largely unexplored. Critics of ODA note that country-level projects are inefficient because they get bogged down in bureaucracy and are a more expensive way of delivering aid because of high priced consultants with steep overheads. The cost of delivering aid theoretically should decrease and efficiency should increase by working at the community level. Remittances go beyond the community level directly to the individual, and, if chan-

Table 1

Remittances from the United States to Developing Countries by Region, 2008 (Billions of \$)

Region	Remittances Received
Latin America and the Caribbean	46.8
Mexico	24.2
East Asia, South Asia and the Pacific	39.2
India	10.6
Philippines	10.4
China	9.8
Sub-Saharan Africa	4.8
Middle East and North Africa	3.9
Europe and Central Asia	2.0
Total	**96.8***

*Variation due to rounding
Source: World Bank, Migration and Remittances Team.

neled correctly, should have a significant development impact.

Economists and policymakers emphasize the need to increase the use of formal transfer channels for remittances. Easing regulation and decreasing the cost of transferring remittances would encourage migrants to send larger amounts of money and receivers of remittances to save and potentially invest some of the money they receive. Additionally, the banks providing the transfer services could use remittance inflows to improve their own credit ratings and the use of formal channels would enable governments to better measure these flows.

Increasing the accessibility of formal remittance-transferring mechanisms is key to improving the efficiency of remittances. Many rural areas in the developing world remain underserved by banks and financial institutions. The entire African continent has as many remittance payout locations as the country of Mexico.[21] World Bank economist Ratha suggests that post offices in developing countries should serve as remittance-receiving locations. In Algeria, over 95% of remittance payouts are received through local post offices.[22]

New research indicates that offering financial products tailored to remitters may be key to mobilizing remittance use for savings and investment. A study supported by the MacArthur Foundation and the Inter-American Development Bank found that while migrants thought that $18 of every $100 remitted should go toward savings, their families wanted to save only $2 of every $100. The study found that demand exists among Salvadorian migrants in the United States for savings accounts in El Salvador that give them control over the account through joint or exclusive ownership. Total savings in households that had access to such accounts increased by 96–136%. The authors conclude that migrants sending money home want a say in how it is used, but lack the financial products to do so.[23]

There is also increasing interest in formal mechanisms to leverage diaspora communities as a source of funds for developing countries through diaspora bonds (see box on Diaspora bonds, p.62). This mechanism may be particularly important in developing countries, specifically within Africa, in which foreign direct investment is limited by lack of credit ratings and other factors.[24]

From leveraging the capital of the diaspora community to securitizing remittances for small entrepreneurs seeking loans, efforts are underway to harness the power of remittances. With remittances expected to remain an important financial flow to developing countries, understanding and capitalizing on these flows remains more important than ever.

An innovative program conducted by TechnoServe in El Salvador to include stable remittance flows in small business loan applications allowed a restaurant owner to expand into the hotel business.

Making Remittances Count

TechnoServe

In 2008, migrants remitted $338 billion to their families in developing countries in an estimated 1.5 billion financial transactions. With only a small portion of remittances going to savings or investments, the potential to catalyze remittances for sustained economic growth has yet to be fully realized. TechnoServe is tapping the power of remittances with a pilot program in El Salvador to help small entrepreneurs leverage remittances to grow their businesses.

TechnoServe, a Washington, DC-based nonprofit economic development organization, is driven by the belief that private enterprise can ignite and sustain economic growth in developing countries. Businessman Ed Bullard founded TechnoServe in 1968 to help entrepreneurs in poor, rural areas of the developing world build businesses that create opportunity and economic growth. Today, TechnoServe works in more than 20 countries in Central and South America, sub-Saharan Africa, and India.

TechnoServe conducted a pilot program in El Salvador from January 2008 to June 2009 to test strategies to leverage remittances to assist small and medium enterprises (SMEs) in accessing credit. The pilot project was funded by the International Fund for Agricultural Development and run in partnership with Microfinance International Corporation (MFIC), a U.S.-based for-profit financial services firm, and Apoyo Integral, the largest microfinance institution in El Salvador.

El Salvador is the perfect environment to test programs to capitalize on remittances because remittances account for nearly 20% of the country's GDP, but only 5–7% of these remittances go to savings or investment. "If remittances can be used for productive purposes then there could be a real economic potential," says Marco Iannone, TechnoServe's deputy

El Salvador is the perfect environment to test programs to capitalize on remittances because remittances account for nearly 20% of the country's GDP, but only 5–7% of these remittances go to savings or investment.

regional director of Latin America and the Caribbean.

The program focused on mechanisms to monetize remittances as declarable sources of income for SMEs seeking credit to demonstrate that remittance-based business loans are viable. TechnoServe identified six SMEs who received regular remittances from the United States and were in need of credit to capitalize on a growth opportunity for their businesses. This included a farmer who wanted to purchase more cattle,

the owner of a small taxi company who wanted to expand his fleet, and a restaurant owner who wanted to expand into the hospitality business.

TechnoServe worked with the business owners to develop detailed business plans. MFIC compiled a comprehensive credit profile for each entrepreneur that included stable remittance flows. TechnoServe then worked with the business owners to apply for a loan from Apoyo Integral.

As a result of the pilot program, four of the six businesses received approval for a loan and two businesses—the restaurant and cattle operation—have received their loans and are in the process of expanding. According to Iannone, the loans these businesses received were 20% to 50% less expensive than traditional loans thanks to the bundling of remittances into the loan applications. He notes that the results point to the potential for greater use of remittances to leverage business capital. "The flow of remittances to a country must be directed to productive purposes to benefit the local economy and maximize development impact," he said. **—Andrew Baltes**

1 Dilip Ratha, "Migration and Remittances Trends 2009," *Migration and Development Brief 11*, World Bank, Migration and Remittances Team, November 3, 2009.

2 Ibid.

3 Dilip Ratha, Sanket Mohapatra, and Ani Silwal, "Outlook for Remittances Flows 2009-2010: Remittances expected to fall by 7-10 percent in 2009," *Migration and Development Brief 10*, World Bank, Migration and Remittances Team, July 13, 2009.

4 Dilip Ratha and Sanket Mohapatra, "Outlook for Remittance Flows 2009-2011," *Migration and Development Brief 9*, World Bank, Migration and Remittances Team, March 23, 2009.

5 "International Conference on Diaspora for Development," World Bank, July 13-14, 2009 http://econ.worldbank.org/WBSITE/EXTERNAL/EXTDEC/EXTDECPROSPECTS/0,,contentMDK:22119861-pagePK:64165401-piPK:64165026 -resourceurlname:%5Be-book%5DInnovative_Financing_for_Development.pdf -theSitePK:476883,00.html (accessed January 14, 2010).

6 "International Forum on Remittances 2009," International Fund for Agricultural Development, October 22-23, 2009, http://www.ifad.org/events/remittances/index.htm (accessed January 14, 2010).

7 "Global Forum On Migration and Development," Civil Society Days, November 2-3, 2009, http://www.gfmd2009.org/discussionPapers .aspx.

8 Dilip Ratha, "Dollars Without Borders: Can the Global Flow of Remittances Survive the Crisis?" *Foreign Affairs*, October 16, 2009.

9 Dilip Ratha, "Migration and Remittances Trends 2009," *Migration and Development Brief 11*, World Bank, Migration and Remittances Team, November 3, 2009.

10 Ibid.

11 Dilip Ratha, Sanket Mohapatra, and Ani Silwal, "Outlook for Remittances Flows 2009-2010: Remittances expected to fall by 7-10 percent in 2009," *Migration and Development Brief 10*, World Bank, Migration and Remittances Team, July 13, 2009.

12 Dilip Ratha, "Migration and Remittances Trends 2009," *Migration and Development Brief 11*, World Bank, Migration and Remittances Team, November 3, 2009.

13 Ibid.

14 Ibid.

15 Ibid.

16 Ibid.

17 Dilip Ratha, Sanket Mohapatra, and Ani Silwal, "Outlook for Remittances Flows 2009-2010: Remittances expected to fall by 7-10 percent in 2009," *Migration and Development Brief 10*, World Bank, Migration and Remittances Team, July 13, 2009.

18 See methodology for a full explanation of calculations.

19 Sanket Mohapatra, George Joseph, and Dilip Ratha, "Remittances and Natural Disasters," Policy Research Working Paper 4872, World Bank, Migration and Remittances Team, June 2009.

20 Claire Adida and Desha Girod. "Do Migrants Improve Their Hometowns?" Stanford University CDDRL Working Paper, April 2009.

21 Robert Meins and Pedro Vasconcelos, "Sending Money Home to Africa—Remittances hold immense untapped potential to the poor," International Fund for Agricultural Development press release, October 22, 2009.

22 Ibid.

23 Dean Yang et al., "Remittances and the Problem of Control: A Field Experiment Among Migrants from El Salvador," August 2009, http://siteresources.worldbank.org/INTINTERNATIONAL/Resources/1572846 -1253029981787/6437326-1253030125818/ Ashraf_Martinez_Yang .pdf (accessed January 14, 2010).

24 Suhas Ketkar and Dilip Ratha, "New Paths to Funding," *Finance and Development, Vol. 46(2)*, June 2009.

U.S. International Philanthropy

Foundations

The Foundation Center's estimates of 2008 international giving by U.S. foundations and of the share of this support benefiting developing countries are based on an analysis of the center's grants sample database and on giving by the nation's nearly 75,600 grantmaking private and community foundations.

The center's 2008 grants sample database includes all of the grants of $10,000 or more authorized or paid by 1,490 of the nation's largest foundations, including 277 corporate foundations. These 164,376 grants totaled $25.3 billion and represented over half of total grant dollars awarded to organizations by all U.S. independent, corporate, community, and grantmaking operating foundations in 2008. International giving by foundations in the sample accounted for the vast majority of total estimated international giving by all U.S. private and community foundations.

Estimates of international foundation giving include all grants awarded to recipients based outside of the United States and its territories and grants to U.S.-based international programs. Grants for developing countries include the subset of awards targeting recipients based in developing countries, U.S.-based and overseas international programs benefiting developing countries, and global health programs. Countries were classified as "developing" based on the 2008 Official Development Assistance Recipient List of the Organization for Economic Cooperation and Development (OECD).

The Foundation Center determined that overall giving by U.S. private and community foundations for international causes was $6,971,552,000: $6,458,553,000 by independent, community, and operating foundations and $512,999,000 from corporate foundations. The Foundation Center estimated the proportion that targeted the developing world based on a detailed analysis of its grants dataset over several years, closely examining the geographic focus of giving by all foundations included in its sample. Foundation giving for developing countries as a share of international giving for non-corporate foundations was estimated to be 67%. Applied to the figure of $6,458,553,000 in overall international giving by non-corporate foundations, the center derived the figure of approximately $4.3 billion for giving by non-corporate foundations for developing countries. International giving for developing countries by corporate foundations was also estimated, but this figure is included in the corporate giving section of the *Index*.

Corporations

The Center for Global Prosperity (CGP) partnered with the Committee Encouraging Corporate Philanthropy (CECP), the Foundation Center, the Urban Institute's Center on Nonprofits and Philanthropy (CNP) and the Partnership for Quality Medical Donations (PQMD) for data on corporate giving for 2008. The CECP is the only international forum focused exclusively on corporate philanthropy and counts 170 business CEOs and chairpersons as members. The PQMD comprises 29 member organizations (nongovernmental organizations and pharmaceutical and medical supply manufacturers) that share a common commitment to advancing effective drug and medical supply donation practices. In addition to information from CECP and PQMD, CGP systematically reviewed giving information

for Fortune 500 companies not reporting through either organization.

A total of 137 companies, including 55 of the Fortune 100, participated in CECP's 2008 Corporate Philanthropy Survey. The survey was conducted under CECP's Corporate Giving Standard (CGS) philanthropy measurement initiative that enables giving professionals to report on their corporate giving. The CGS is a unique industry tool that provides immediate, on-demand reporting and benchmarking while preserving essential anonymity for individual company data.

For the 2009 survey on 2008 giving, CECP once again included questions on corporate giving to the developing world specifically for the *Index*. CECP received a total of 43 responses to these questions, with 35 corporations reporting donations to the developing world. Of the 35 companies that reported giving, 5 were pharmaceutical companies that only reported direct cash giving ($9,565,107) and foundation cash ($29,224,381). The remaining 30 non-pharmaceutical companies reported $48,323,719 in direct cash giving, $59,316,721 in giving through corporate foundations, and $20,580,162 in in-kind giving at fair market value for a total of $167,010,090.

The Foundation Center through its survey of corporate foundations found that corporate foundations gave $512,999,000 internationally. Based on the Foundation Centers calculations, an estimated 53% or $272,148,000 of this went to developing countries specifically.

Private and voluntary organizations (PVOs) with a tax year ending 12/2008 filed the "new" IRS Form 990 which allowed the CNP to base estimates on the amount of "In-Kind Drugs and Medical Supplies" reported in Schedule M, Line 20 to be $4,901,016,273 donated to them by corporations. This was the first year that 990s requested in-kind information be separately documented by type of in-kind contribution. CGP substituted the CNP number this year because the PQMD number used in past editions of the Index was not available for 2008. Schedule F is also used to identify assistance given to developing nations and regions (excluding assistance to domestic and developed nations). Most PVOs report "Wholesale Value," "Market Value," "Comparable Sales," "Red Book," or other published sources for valuation method in Line 20 of Schedule M.

Added to the in-kind donations of pharmaceuticals and medical supplies for international relief and development are the overhead costs incurred mostly by corporations donating these in-kind contributions. Based on their members' consensus, PQMD estimates that transport, insurance and handling costs add 10% or $490,101,627 to donors' costs. Duties, taxes and tariffs accounted for 18% or $882,182,929. Storage, distribution and in-country transport cost an additional 15% or $735,152,441. When the aforementioned overhead costs are applied to the $4,901,016,273, total in-kind donations by corporations for 2008 amount to $7,008,453,270.

Finally, CGP staff conducted an extensive review of Fortune 500 companies not reporting through CECP. CGP reviewed annual reports, conducted Internet searches, and contacted some companies by phone, tallying a total of $273,982,019 in cash and in-kind giving from the companies for which figures were available.

Together, $167,010,090 from CECP research, $272,148,000 from the Foundation Center, $7,008,453,270 from in-kind corporate donation data to PVOs, and $273,982,019 from CGP's own research amounted to a total of $7.7 billion in U.S. corporate giving to the developing world.

Private and Voluntary Organizations

The CGP once again collaborated with the Urban Institute's Center on Nonprofits and Philanthropy (CNP) to determine the dollar value of international development assistance projects run by private and voluntary organizations (PVOs). Building on its earlier research on international PVOs, the CNP examined approximately 6,200 IRS Form 990 information returns that PVOs filed with the Internal Revenue Service, primarily for Fiscal Year 2008. (2007 Form 990s were used when 2008 IRS Form 990s were not available.)

The CNP also used information from the *USAID U.S. PVO Registry* (also known as the *USAID U.S. Voluntary Agencies list*, or *VolAg*) list for organizations that did not file Form 990s (2007 data as of February, 2010 are available at http://www.pvo.net/usaid/index.html). These were primarily religious organizations not required to file Form 990s and newly registered PVOs with international development activities. The data set of 73,000 nonprofit organizations newly registered with the IRS in 2008 was processed using an automated classification program to identify organizations with possible international development activities. Domestic organizations, such as community theaters and neighborhood associations, were excluded. Environmental, human service or healthcare organizations that could have both domestic and international activities were retained. To align the CNP data set with CGP specifications, the CNP removed all organizations that primarily supported activities in the United States or other developed countries. The programs of organizations showing possible international development activity were then reviewed manually.

To differentiate international and domestic program activities, expenses and contributions for these organizations, the CNP reviewed the organizations' Form 990s, web sites, and annual reports, and the *VolAg* registry to determine the international to domestic ratio for the 4,700 largest organizations. Total expenditures per region were used when available from the 1,800 PVOs filing the new Schedule F (Statement of Activities Outside the United States) of the revised Form 990; expenditures per region were estimated from program service descriptions and annual reports for 700 others. The organizations reviewed by CNP accounted for approximately 91% of the total private contributions.

For the remaining smaller organizations, the CNP estimated that contributions for international activities represented 95–98% of total contributions (the precise percentage varied depending on the size of the organization). The CNP then applied these percentages to the total private contributions, including cash and in-kind contributions, of these smaller organizations to determine the total amount of PVO contributions for international activities.

To eliminate double-counting that would occur if foundation grants to PVOs were included in the private contributions reported by the PVOs in their 990s or the *VolAg*, the CNP prepared a list of the 200 largest PVOs and the Foundation Center matched this list with the grants received by the organizations and determined whether the grants were intended for developing countries. Then the total amount of international foundation grants to U.S.-based organizations for development purposes, approximately $915 million, was subtracted from the estimate of private contributions for development and relief calculated from the 2008 PVO database total, approximately $17.6 billion, resulting in a subtotal of almost $16.7 billion.

To eliminate double-counting of corporate contributions of pharmaceuticals and other medical supplies or equipment that are accounted for in the Corporations section of the *Index*, CNP reviewed the *VolAg* data, IRS Form 990s, web sites and annual reports for all organizations reporting significant in-kind contributions of goods and that were active in health development and assistance work or that had major health-related activities. PVOs filing the revised Form 990 with Schedule M (Noncash Contributions) were examined for reporting large in-kind contributions of drugs and medical supplies (Line 20). These organizations reported a total of nearly $5 billion in in-kind contributions of pharmaceuticals or other medical supplies. This amount was deducted from the private contribution subtotal of almost $16.7 billion, resulting in $11.8 billion in private contributions received by U.S. PVOs and spent for international development and relief.

Volunteer Time

The *Index* estimate of the value of U.S. volunteer time for developing countries in 2008 is based on data taken from the Current Population Survey (CPS) and Independent Sector's estimated dollar value of volunteer time. The CPS is a monthly survey of about 50,000 households conducted by the Bureau of the Census for the Bureau of Labor Statistics. As with the estimate of the value of U.S. international volunteer time for 2007, CGP based the 2008 estimate on two categories of respondents to the volunteer supplement: those who volunteered outside of the United States and those who volunteered in the United States for organizations that support international development assistance.

The CPS tallies individual volunteer time spent abroad and, separately, the type of organization for which individuals volunteer. Thus, CGP was able to determine how many people volunteered abroad and how much time they spent doing so and how many people volunteered for U.S.-based international organizations and how much time they spent doing so. For the second category, the CPS does not provide a breakdown of where the volunteering time was spent—abroad or in the United States. Because of this, survey respondents who volunteered for a U.S.-based international organization and said they volunteered abroad might be double counted. To avoid this, CGP staff excluded the individuals who volunteered for an international organization and who also volunteered abroad. This resulted in two distinct groups of

volunteers: those who volunteered abroad and those who volunteered in the United States in support of international development causes.

CGP staff calculated the value of U.S. volunteers' time spent abroad by multiplying the 2008 estimated hourly value of volunteer time by the estimate of total volunteer hours abroad as calculated from the 2008 volunteer supplement data, which asked respondents: "Considering all of the volunteer work you have done since September 1st of last year, about how much of it was done abroad: all or almost all; more than half; about half; less than half; or very little?" CGP staff assigned percentage values (95%, 75%, 50%, 25%, and 5% respectively) to each of these categories to calculate the numbers of hours served overseas. Based on Bureau of Labor statistics figures, Independent Sector estimated the dollar value of a volunteer's time to be $20.25 per hour in 2008. Multiplying the 123,873,007 U.S. volunteer hours contributed overseas by the hourly wage of $20.25 brings the dollar value of U.S. volunteer hours contributed overseas to $2,508,428,399.

To calculate the value of time volunteered in support of international development assistance causes in the United States, CGP staff identified CPS respondents who served with one or more international organizations and totaled the hours they served across all international organizations, removing those who had volunteered overseas. There were 462,979 volunteers in this category in 2008. This figure multiplied by the 120.5 average hours volunteered by this group in 2008 yields a total of 55,770,450 hours. Multiplying 55,770,450 by the hourly wage of $20.25 brings the dollar value of U.S. volunteer hours contributed on U.S. soil for international development causes to $1,129,351,619.

By adding the economic value of U.S. volunteers' time dedicated to international causes at home to the economic value of those who volunteered abroad, CGP estimates the total value of U.S. volunteer time for international causes in 2008 to be $3,637,780,018. The estimate for 2008 volunteer time is higher than the 2007 figure for two reasons. While the number of volunteers who traveled abroad slightly decreased, the number of individuals who volunteered for an international organization in the US increased by 40%. Second, the value of an hour of volunteer time increased from $19.51 in 2007 to $20.25 in 2008. The increase in the value of volunteer time is likely to be the main cause of the increase in the 2008 volunteer contributions to international causes.

Universities and Colleges

The CGP once again used data from the Institute for International Education's (IIE) annual *Open Doors* survey, which gathers information on international students in the United States and on U.S. students abroad. *Open Doors* covers the 671,616 international students who studied in the United States in the 2008–2009 academic year and includes cost breakdowns of their tuition and fees, living expenses, and their sources of support.

Open Doors compiles information on all international students coming to the U.S. from all regions of the world. For the 2010 *Index*, CGP again refined the regional analysis to deduct from the total number of students from each predominantly developing world region the number of students who came to the U.S. from the few developed countries within the region. CGP determined that 61% of international students came to the United States from the developing world by calculating the proportion of students from developing world countries relative to the worldwide total.

The analysis for *Open Doors* accounted for various cost categories of international students in the United States to produce a total for all expenses for all international students in the United States in 2007–2008 of $24,604,700,000. Among the sources of these funds were personal and family contributions, home governments, foreign private sponsors, international organizations, U.S. sources, and employment. According to *Open Doors*, the proportion of this $24.6 billion total that came from U.S. sources was $6,948,000,000. Also, according to *Open Doors*, the U.S. government was the primary source of funding for 0.6% of international students, which yields a contribution of $41,688,000. Subtracting $41,688,000 in U.S. government support from $6,948,500,000 yields $6,906,312,000 in support from U.S. sources other than the U.S. government. Multiplying this figure by the 61% that represents the portion of students from the developing world yields a total of $4,223,403,275 or $4.2 billion for contributions to students from the developing world. While we removed the number of students whose primary source of funding is the U.S. government, the remaining students' funds came from U.S. private sponsors and host university or college funds. The IIE does not provide information on what portion of the university/college funding comes from the U.S. government. However, the IIE speculates that a large portion of the doctoral students receive funding from U.S. government sources such as the National Science Foundation or the National Institute of Health. To be conservative, CGP found the ratio of all international students in the U.S. who are in non-doctoral programs, which in 2008 amounted to 41.2%, and applied this ratio to the $4.2 billion total for non-governmental U.S. funding to students from developing nations. This yielded a final estimate of $1.7 billion. Thus the final estimate, a likely under-estimate, only includes U.S. private funding for non-doctoral students studying in the U.S. from developing countries.

The Institute for International Education's methodology for the survey includes a country classification system that organizes places of origin into regional groupings based on the U.S. Department of State's definition of world regions and states. The survey defines an international student as "an individual who is enrolled for courses at a higher education institution in the United States on a temporary visa." The survey pool consists of 2,866 regionally accredited U.S. institutions and is updated and refreshed regularly using the Integrated Postsecondary Education Data System (IPEDS) (produced by the U.S. Department of Education) and the U.S. Department of Homeland Security's SEVIS (Student and Exchange Visitor Information System). The overall institutional response rate for 2007–08 was 66.1%, or 1,895 institutions; nearly 97% of responding institutions reported enrollment of international students.

Religious Organizations

The Center for Global Prosperity (CGP) has continued its ground-breaking work on U.S. giving for international relief and development by U.S. congregations with a new survey for *Index 2010*, measuring giving in 2008. This year, the Urban Institute's National Center for Charitable Statistics (NCCS) teamed up with the Social and Economic Sciences Research Center (SESRC) at Washington State University to conduct a national survey on the scope and magnitude of congregational support for international relief and development.

The Urban Institute's Congregational Survey consisted of all religious congregations in the United States. Urban Institute used American Church List to select a stratified random sample to ensure congregations of different sizes, denominations, and geographic areas were included in the study. Churches with larger memberships were given a higher probability of selection. Each sampled congregation was asked about their overseas donations for relief and development in 2008. The final questionnaire was designed to be administered either by mail, by web, or by phone and consisted of four sections: 1) U.S.-Based Organizations, 2) Overseas-Based Organizations, Ministries, & Long-Term Missions, 3) Short-Term Missions, and 4) Organization Background.

The sample size of the congregation survey was 1,200; we received 576 responses. The response rate was 51%, which was calculated by including all completed and partially completed questionnaires and followed the guidelines from AAPOR (American Association of Public Opinion Research) on how to treat ineligible organizations, such as congregations with disconnected phone numbers. A hot deck imputation procedure was used for partially completed questionnaires and surveys that had missing information on total dollar amounts. In a hot deck imputation, the value reported by a respondent for a particular question is given or donated to a "similar" organization whose respondent failed to respond to that question. The hot deck approach replaces missing data with plausible values, which is why it is the most common method used to assign values for missing responses in organizational surveys.

Results were weighted to adjust for non-response, disproportionate sampling by size, and the estimated 335,000 congregations in the United States, a number recognized by scholars in the field to be in the middle range of estimates. The survey focused exclusively on international relief and development; support for evangelism, church planting, discipleship, and street evangelism was explicitly removed from the totals for overseas-based organizations and missions.

The survey determined that 1) an estimated 242,230 congregations gave a total of approximately $6.2 billion to U.S.-based development and relief organizations; 2) an estimated 149,179 congregations contributed a total of $4.5 billion directly to programs in foreign countries including congregations that supported longer term mission trips for relief and development; and 3) an estimated 107,403 congregations financially supported short-term mission

trips to foreign countries by providing $1.1 billion in support including participant contributions. The $6.2 billion given to U.S.-based development and relief organizations was excluded from our estimate of religious giving since we included giving to these organizations in our numbers for PVOs.

The congregation survey data comprises all U.S. religious denominations. Combined with data from the Church of Jesus Christ of Latter-Day Saints and the Billy Graham Center at Wheaton College on giving by Protestant mission agencies (denominational boards, nondenominational societies and other organizations involved in overseas development assistance), the *Index* continues to provide a unique look at overall religious giving by U.S. religious institutions.

The Church of Jesus Christ of Latter Day Saints (LDS) shared with the CGP its data on assistance for 2008. LDS congregations gave a total of $68.8 million dollars with roughly equal amounts of cash versus in-kind donations. Since no LDS congregations were included in the Urban Institute congregations survey results, the LDS total was added separately.

The Billy Graham Center at Wheaton College's most recently published *Mission Handbook* is a study of giving to 700 U.S. mission agencies (Protestant religious organizations engaged in missions overseas) and was based on data from 2005. In 2005, the Billy Graham Center reported a total of $5.24 billion in revenue for mission agencies from grants, individual giving, bequests, and other sources. The Graham Center provided us with a new total giving number of approximately $5.7 billion for its most recent survey covering 2008 giving, which will be published in spring 2010 — after our *Index* goes to press. This number was used to adjust the 2005 data to 2008 levels. By comparing 2005 revenues to 2008 revenues we found an 8.77% growth in revenues from all Billy Graham Center organizations.

To eliminate double-counting of organizations in the *Mission Handbook* that also filed IRS Form 990s or completed the USAID VOLAG survey, the NCCS matched its database with the Billy Graham Center's organizations. It found that approximately 40% of the organizations in the Billy Graham Center's *Mission Handbook* Survey, representing 55% of the 2005 revenue — $2.89 billion of the $5.24 billion — reported data through one of these other sources. These organizations were, therefore, excluded from the religious giving estimate, leaving an unduplicated amount of $2.35 billion from organizations reporting solely to the Billy Graham Center.

To estimate the Billy Graham Center's unique contribution for 2008 (since we do not have the complete results of this survey, but only the total of $5.7 billion), we applied the percentage growth increase of 8.77% to this $2.35 billion to arrive at $2.56 billion for the total contributions to the developing world by the Protestant mission organizations in the Billy Graham Center survey for 2008 that did not report elsewhere.

Due to data limitations, it is not possible to completely disaggregate evangelism activities from relief and development activities in the Billy Graham Center data. For this reason, the $2.56 billion might represent an overestimation; however, the Urban Institute's Congregational Survey and data from the Church of Jesus Christ of Latter-day Saints (LDS), which make up the majority of our religious giving number, include only funds spent strictly on relief and development. The private giving figures from the Urban Institute's congregation survey ($5.6 billion), the Billy Graham Center ($2.56 billion) and the LDS ($68.8 million) result in a total of $8.23 billion in religious giving.

International Philanthropy Outside the United States

Denmark

To obtain private giving estimates for Denmark, CGP partnered with Stein Brothers AB, a Swedish research and consulting firm. Peter Stein, CEO of Stein Brothers AB, collected data on Danish international giving in 2008 in two areas: giving by international development PVOs and corporate giving.

The estimate for PVO private giving is based on data from Projektråd-givningen, an umbrella body for Danish international development PVOs, and data from the Danish Ministry of Foreign Affairs. Using both these sources, it was possible to identify ten Danish PVOs that account for more than 70% of all private philanthropy to the developing world that is channeled through PVOs in Denmark. The remaining 25–28% is distributed between some 50 organizations. By analyzing each annual report from the ten PVOs and through follow-up contact, it was established that they gave 598 million DKK or $120.4 million to the developing world.

Acquiring an estimate of what Danish corporations gave to the developing world in 2008 was difficult because Denmark has few large multinational corporations. The corporate giving figure for 2008 is based on what one Danish multinational gave to the developing world. This amounted to 66.1 million DKK or $13.3 million.

Together these categories total 664 million DKK. Using the conversion rate of 4.967 published by the Financial Management Service of the United States Department of the Treasury to convert Danish Krone to U.S. dollars provided an estimate of $133.7 million in Danish private giving to the developing world. The increase in private giving from 2007 to 2008 is largely due to an increase in contributions from Danish PVOs.

Finland

To obtain private giving estimates for Finland, CGP partnered with Stein Brothers AB, a Swedish research and consulting firm. Peter Stein, CEO of Stein Brothers AB, collected data on Finnish international giving in 2008 in two areas: giving by international development PVOs and corporate giving.

Approximately 80% of private philanthropy to the developing world channeled through Finnish PVOs is accounted for by the 10 largest PVOs. Having identified these organizations through the Finnish Ministry of Foreign Affairs, Stein Brothers AB sent out a questionnaire to each of them asking how much their private income was for the year 2008. Each organization's annual report was also analyzed and follow-up contact was made. Private income for these PVOs amounted to €28.3 million or $40.1 million in 2008. Additionally, Stein Brothers AB contacted the Service Centre for Development Cooperation (KEPA, www.kepa.fi), a service base for Finnish PVOs interested in development work and global issues, to obtain additional information on 2008 PVO self-financing for projects done in cooperation with the Ministry of Foreign Affairs of Finland. According to KEPA, the total amount of money that Finnish PVOs contributed on their own was €7.9 or $11.2 million in 2008.

Corporate giving data was collected by sending out an e-mail survey to the five largest Finnish multinational corporations. The questionnaire outlined the purpose of the study and asked how much the corporation gave to the developing world in 2008. The relevant corporate philanthropic contributions were €8.6 million or $12.2 million.

Together these categories total €44.8 million. Using the conversion rate of 0.706 published by the Financial Management Service of the United States Department of the Treasury to convert Euro to U.S. dollars provided an estimate $63.5 million in Finnish private giving to the developing world.

France

To obtain our private giving estimate for France, the CGP was able to obtain an update on French individual giving to developing countries. Because 2008 data on French corporate giving and bequests was not available, CGP used data from 2007. Thus French giving to international development consisted of three sources: corporate giving, bequests, and individual giving.

Corporate giving data were taken from a corporate giving survey by L'Association pour le Développement du Mécénat Industriel et Commercial, a French corporate sponsorship organization, and the market research firm CSA. The data were based on a sample of 750 French corporations of 20 or more employees. An estimated 15% of total French corporate giving was internationally orientated. Using a 2007 conversion rate of 0.7463 published by the Financial Management Service of the United States Department of the Treasury to convert Euros to U.S. dollars, this amounted to €375 million or $502.5 million.

Studies by the Centre d'Etudes et de Recherches sur la Philanthropie, a Paris based think tank that conducts research on French philanthropy, show that bequests from individuals rose to €500 million in 2007. Five percent, or €25 million, of this went to international charities. Using the above 2007 conversion rate this amounted to $33.5 million.

To estimate individual giving, CGP used data commissioned by Charistar, an Amsterdam based advisory agency with a focus on nonprofit organizations. Dr. Wiepking from the Vrije Universiteit Amsterdam Department of Philanthropy designed the questionnaire and supervised the fieldwork, a household survey of French giving, which was conducted by TNS (tnsglobal.com), an international global data collection agency. One of the questions on the survey asked, "What is the total amount that your household donated in 2008 to charitable organizations active in the field of international assistance?" Sur-

vey results and data analysis found that 18.9% of French households gave to international assistance with an average donation of €114.0 or $161.4, using a 2008 conversion rate of 0.706 published by the Financial Management Service of the United States Department of the Treasury to convert Euros to U.S. dollars. In total, French individual giving to international assistance organizations amounted to €330.8 million or $468.6 in 2008.

Together these three categories total $1.0 billion in French private giving to the developing world. This figure contains the most recent 2007 data on corporations and bequests, and the most recent 2008 data on individual giving in France.

Italy

To obtain our private giving estimate for Italy, the CGP partnered with Instituto per la Ricerca Sociale (IRS), an independent, non-profit research organization based in Italy. IRS has been involved in research on a variety of social issues for over 30 years. To estimate the value of private contributions to international development, IRS collected giving data from certified PVOs and banking foundations.

According to Italian law certified Italian PVOs can obtain approval for the management of International Aid by the Ministry of Foreign Affairs. In order to obtain this certification the institution has to have a mission aimed at "international cooperation for developing countries" and is responsible for assigning all collected funds to international activities. IRS identified these PVOs from the "Report on social economy" produced by Institutio Nazionale di Statistica and Consiglio Nazionale dell'Economia e del Lavoro. IRS identified 241 PVOs that work in international aid in 2008. The total funding to these PVOs amounted to €1,056,077,000 or $1,495,860,000 of which €647.8 million or $918 million came from the public sector, while funding from private sources amounted to 39%. In total, the IRS estimates that private contributions to these PVOs amounted to €409.0 million or $579.3 million.

Italian banking foundations stem from a long tradition of Italian savings banks playing an active role in socially responsible activities. To obtain the value that banking foundations contributed to international development in 2008, IRS contacted the Banking Foundations Association (ACRI) and analyzed its annual reports. IRS found that in 2008 these foundations contributed a total of €1,277.0 million or $1,809.0 million in donations to all sectors. Based on IRS assessment, an estimated €2.7 million or $3.8 million of these donations were transferred to developing countries directly. These funds do not include money transferred to Italian PVOs.

Together these categories total €411.7 million. Using the conversion rate of 0.706 published by the Financial Management Service of the United States Department of the Treasury to convert Euro to U.S. dollars provided an estimate $583.1 million in Italian private giving to the developing world.

Luxembourg

The private giving estimate for Luxembourg is based on research performed by the Center for Global Prosperity staff. We researched 62 of the largest members of Le Cercle de Coopération des ONG de Développement, the only international development PVO umbrella group in Luxembourg. By analyzing their annual reports and through direct contact with them, we were able to establish private giving numbers for 16 of the organizations.

Their private income for 2008 totaled €13,808,327. Using the conversion rate of 0.706 published by the Financial Management Service of the United States Department of the Treasury to convert Euros to U.S. dollars provided an estimate of $19.6 in private giving to the developing world from Luxembourg.

The Netherlands

The private giving estimate for the Netherlands is based on the 2009 edition of the biannual report *Geven in Nederland* produced by the Vrije Universiteit Amsterdam, which provides data for 2007. The report includes giving in the category of "international aid" from five sources: households, bequests, foundations, corporations and lotteries. According to the report, households gave €298 million, or $399.4 million, to international aid causes in cash and in-kind donations; €41 million, or $54.9 million, came from bequests; €17 million, or $22.8 million, came from foundations; €70 million, or $93.8 million, came from corporate gifts and sponsorship; and €94 million, or $126 million, came from lotteries.

Together these categories total €520 million. Using a 2007 conversion rate of 0.7462 published by the Financial Management Service of the United States Department of the Treasury to convert Euros to U.S. dollars provided an estimate of $696.9 million in Dutch private giving to the developing world.

New Zealand

The private giving number for New Zealand is based on data from the Council for International Development (CID), an umbrella body for New Zealand's major international development PVOs. According to CID's 2009 annual report, in 2008 private income for its members came to NZ$123.6 million, or $92.9 million using the 2008 conversion rate of 1.33. NZ$113.1 million or $85.0 million of this was from donations from the public and NZ$10.5 million or $7.9 million came from contracted work, foundation grants, grants from parent organizations, and the sale of goods.

Norway

To obtain private giving estimates for Norway, CGP partnered with Stein Brothers AB, a Swedish research and consulting firm. Peter Stein, CEO of Stein Brothers AB, collected data on Norwegian international giving in 2008 by measuring giving by international development PVOs.

To estimate giving by PVOs, Stein contacted the Norwegian Agency for Development Cooperation (NORAD) to identify the top 10 largest Norwegian PVOs. Stein reviewed the annual reports of each PVO and when necessary contacted the organization directly. By analyzing data, he estimated that Norwegian PVOs gave 1386.7 million NOK. Using the conversion rate of 5.3 published by the Financial Management Service of the United States Department of the Treasury to convert NOK to U.S. dollars provided an estimate of $261.6 million in private giving from Norwegian PVOs to the developing world.

While Norwegian corporations also give to philanthropic activities in the developing world, they do so solely by giving to international PVOs. Thus in order to avoid double counting, it can be assumed that any Norwegian corporate contribution is included in the PVO figure. Therefore, total Norwegian giving amounted to $261.6 million.

Portugal

The private giving estimate for Portugal is based on research performed by CGP staff. Using Plataforma Portuguesa das ONGD, the largest Portuguese international development organization umbrella groups, as a resource, CGP researched 55 of the largest international development PVOs and foundations. By analyzing their annual reports and through direct contact with the organizations, CGP was able to establish private giving numbers to the developing world for 12 of the organizations. Their private income for 2008 totaled €6,387,186. Using the conversion rate of 0.706 published by the Financial Management Service of the United States Department of the Treasury to convert Euros to U.S. dollars provided an estimate of $9.0 million in Portuguese private giving to the developing world.

Spain

The private giving estimate for Spain is based on a report by Coordinadora de ONG Para El Desarrollo España, a Spanish association of 100 international development organizations. Coordinadora de ONG Para El Desarrollo España gathered its information by surveying all its member organizations. The CGP estimate represents the private income for these organizations in 2007, the latest year for which data are available. Private income for these organizations came from five main sources: €127.2 million or $170.4 million in regular donations and fees; €104.6 million or $140.2 million in one-time donations; €35.4 million or $47.5 million from private enterprises; €25.7 million or $34.4 million from the sale of fair trade products and merchandising; and €12.5 million or $16.7 million from other private funds.

Together these categories total €305.4 million. Using a 2007 conversion rate of 0.7463 published by the Financial Management Service of the United States Department of the Treasury to convert Euros to U.S. dollars provided an estimate of $409.2 million in Spanish private giving to the developing world.

Sweden

To obtain private giving estimates for Sweden, CGP partnered with Stein Brothers AB, a Swedish research and consulting firm. Peter Stein, CEO of Stein Brothers AB, collected data on Swedish international giving in 2008 in two areas: giving by international development PVOs and foundations and corporate giving.

To estimate giving by PVOs and foundations, Stein used data from the Swedish International Development Cooperation Agency and from the Swedish Committee on Fundraising Organizations, which holds comprehensive data on all PVOs and foundations based in Sweden. By analyzing data from both this source and by using individual PVO and foundation annual reports, he estimated that Swedish PVOs and foundations gave 1105.6 million SEK or $177.2 million. This number has increased from the number reported in 2007 due to an increase in contributions from PVOs reported in *Index* 2009 and due to the inclusion of additional Swedish NGOs for which data was unavailable for last year's *Index*.

Corporate giving data was collected by sending out an e-mail survey to the 20 largest Swedish exporters. This group includes most of the largest Swedish multinational corporations that together account for more than 56% of Swedish exports. The questionnaire outlined the purpose of the study and asked how much the corporation gave to the developing world in 2008. The companies that replied collectively gave 227.2 million SEK or $36.4 million to the developing world. None of this money was channeled through Swedish PVOs or foundations. This figure does not count in-kind giving, technical assistance and volunteering.

Together these categories total 1332.8 million SEK. Using the conversion rate of 6.24 published by the Financial Management Service of the United States Department of the Treasury to convert Swedish Krona to U.S. dollars provided an estimate of $213.6 million in Swedish private giving to the developing world.

Switzerland

To obtain private giving estimates for Switzerland, CGP partnered with Stein Brothers AB, a Swedish research and consulting firm. Peter Stein, CEO of Stein Brothers AB, collected data on Swiss international giving in 2008 in two areas: giving by international development PVOs and corporate giving.

There are over 300 registered PVOs in Switzerland. To estimate private giving by PVOs Stein used data from the Swiss Federal Department of Foreign Affairs, which conducts an annual report survey of 339 Swiss PVOs. Stein Brothers AB also analyzed the annual reports of additional PVOs not included in the survey. By analyzing data from both these sources and by using individual PVO and foundation annual reports, he estimated that Swiss PVOs and foundations gave 473.5 million CHF or $438.0 million.

Corporate giving data was collected by contacting and analyzing data from the top 20 Swiss corporations. Companies that replied collectively gave 89.9 million CHF or $83.2 million to the developing world. None of this money was channeled through Swiss PVOs. This figure does not count in-kind giving, technical assistance and volunteering.

Together these categories total 563.4 million CHF. Using the 2008 conversion rate of 1.081 published by the Financial Management Service of the United States Department of the Treasury to convert Swiss Francs to U.S. dollars provided an estimate of $521.2 million in Swiss private giving to the developing world.

United Kingdom

To obtain our private giving estimate for the United Kingdom, the CGP again partnered with GuideStar Data Services (GDS). GuideStar holds data on all charities registered in England and Wales, including activities, area of benefit, income and income from private sources.

GDS identified all those UK charities that work in the area of "overseas aid/ famine relief," one of 13 categories by which charities define their activities when they register with the UK Charity Commission. This subset was further narrowed by removing charities that are not working in countries classified by the OECD as developing countries or working in regions of the world known to include a high proportion of developed countries. Charities excluded were those known to be working in the following countries or regions: Russia, Israel, Romania, Bulgaria, Latvia, Lithuania, Estonia, Slovakia, Slovenia, and Cyprus. The following countries were excluded because of lack of charity data: Suriname and Myanmar.

For the remaining charities identified as working in overseas aid/famine relief in developing countries, GDS provided CGP with information on the total number of such organizations, the total income of these organizations, and the total private income of these organizations.

Because charities are not required to file their income and expenditure figures for up to ten months after the end of their first year of operation, there is no financial information available for some new charities. Charities with an annual income of less than £10,000 ($19,773) are not required to submit detailed accounts and therefore no information is available from these charities about the proportion of income that comes from private sources. However, the total income of these charities is less than half a percent of the population of charities analyzed so their exclusion has little effect on the overall private giving number.

Total private income for UK charities working in overseas aid/famine relief amounted to £3,457,909,034 in 2008 raised by 7,615 charities. Using a conversion rate of 0.5525 published by the Financial Management Service of the United States Department of the Treasury to convert British pounds to U.S. dollars provided an estimate of $6.3 billion in UK private giving to the developing world.

Global Remittances

The World Bank's 2006 bilateral matrix, which is the only comprehensive and comparable source of all bilateral remittance flows, was used to calculate remittance transfers from OECD donor countries to DAC recipient countries in 2008. Dilip Ratha and William Shaw of the World Bank created the bilateral matrix version 4 by allocating remittances received by each developing country among the countries of destination of its migrant nationals (for a complete discussion of how the matrix was complied, including the formulas used to calculate remittances, see Dilip Ratha and William Shaw, *South-South Migration and Remittances*, World Bank Working Paper No. 102, 2007, Appendix A and Appendix B).

The 2006 matrix data ("Bilateral remittance estimates using migrant stocks, destination country incomes, and source country incomes.") were used to estimate remittance intensities (the share of remittance inflows from a specific donor country), which were then projected onto 2008 remittance inflow data of receiving countries to calculate the total remittance inflow of the recipient country (this method assumes that migrant stocks will remain unchanged between 2006 and 2008).

The following formula was used to calculate remittances received by the receiving country (country "i") from the sending country (country "j"):

$$\text{Remittance}(i,j\ 2008) = [\text{Remittances}(i,j\ 2006)/\text{Remittances}(i\ 2008)]*\text{Remittances}(i\ 2008)$$

where i is the remittance receiving country and j is the remittance sending country.

$\text{Remittances}(i,j\ 2006)$ is the remittance received by country i from country j in 2006.

$\text{Remittances}(i\ 2006)$ is the total remittances received by country i in 2006.

$\text{Remittances}(i\ 2008)$ is the total remittances received by country i in 2008.

Total 2008 remittance inflow data by country were calculated by the World Bank based on the International Monetary Fund's *Balance of Payments Statistics Yearbook 2008* and data released from central banks, national statistical agencies, and World Bank country desks.

Our estimate is likely to be conservative due to limitations in data. Bilateral matrix data were not available for a number of DAC recipient countries: Afghanistan, Angola, Barbados, Bhutan, Burundi, Central African Republic, Chad, DRC, Cuba, Djibouti, Equatorial Guinea, Eritrea, Iraq, Liberia, Marshall Islands, Mayotte, Micronesia, Myanmar, Oman, Palau, Somalia, Timor-Leste, Turkmenistan, Uzbekistan, Vanuatu, Zimbabwe.

ACKNOWLEDGEMENTS

Index 2010 benefitted from the research, assistance and counsel of a number of organizations representing the highest expertise in their fields. These organizations conducted research, provided data, assisted in designing methodologies and in resolving methodological challenges, and provided authoritative information about developments in the field of private sector philanthropy for developing countries. The information and insights they provided resulted in a document that places unique information in important contexts.

The Foundation Center was again our partner on foundation giving. The Foundation Center conducts research on foundation trends, and operates education and training programs that help nonprofit organizations obtain resources, maintains a robust web site, and provides thousands of people annually with access to free resources in its five library/learning centers, as well as in its 400 funding information centers. The center worked collaboratively with the Urban Institute to ensure accurate information about PVO contributions. We are grateful to Steve Lawrence for his diligence in providing timely and comprehensive data, for his collegial cooperation with the Urban Institute, and for his ongoing guidance on foundation giving.

We are grateful for the generous cooperation of the Committee Encouraging Corporate Philanthropy (CECP), the only international forum with a mission focused exclusively on corporate philanthropy. CECP's director, Margaret Coady, designed and administered a special supplemental survey on CECP member organization giving to the developing world. We are also again grateful for CECP Executive Director Charles Moore's support of the partnership. Lori Warrens, executive director of the Partnership for Quality Medical Donations (PQMD), another partner in the corporations section, provided data and invaluable information on the scope and reach of in-kind medical donations of pharmaceuticals and medical supplies.

Our partner on giving by PVOs was once again the Urban Institute's Center for Nonprofits and Philanthropy (CNP). We are grateful for the rigor and depth of research conducted by Tom Pollak, Timothy Triplett, and Jon Durnford. Pollak and his colleagues have been unstintingly generous with their time and advice. In addition to providing PVO data, they oversaw the religious giving survey and provided essential support in accounting for overlap in giving among the foundation, PVO and religious organization sectors. We are also grateful to CNP Director Elizabeth Boris for her support and counsel.

We thank Institute of International Education (IIE) Research Manager Patricia Chow for her assistance in analyzing the complex data on international students in the U.S. contained in IIE's *Open Doors*. IIE is a world leader in international exchange and training; its counsel has been invaluable in identifying methodologies that provide unique information for the *Index*. We are also grateful to IIE Executive Vice President Peggy Blumenthal for her continuing counsel.

Tom Pollak and Timothy Triplett of the Urban Institute's National Center for Charitable Statistics (NCCS) teamed up with the Social and Economic Sciences Research Center (SESRC) at Washington State University to conduct a new national survey on the scope and magnitude of congregational support for international relief and development. We are again grateful for the advice and assistance of Kenneth Gill, Linda Weber and Scott Moreau at the Billy Graham Center and Eric Wunderlich of The Church of Jesus Christ of Latter-day Saints for additional information on religious giving.

The CGP is grateful to Nathan Dietz at the Corporation for National and Community Service for guiding us through the Current Population Survey's volunteer supplement and pointing us to the methodological applications that would yield information essential to the analyses.

We would like to thank our international research partners for their help in researching data and trends on private giving outside the United States. With the help of Peter Stein, we were able to publish the first private giving estimates of philanthropy to the developing world from Scandinavia. We would also like to thank Charles Sellen for his expertise, which allowed us to obtain a more comprehensive French private giving number. For the French number we also received help from Pamela Wiepking from the European Research Network on Philanthropy and Edith Bruder from Centre d'Etude et de Recherche sur la Philanthropie. For our UK private giving research, we would like to thank Sally Bagwell, account manager, and Diarra Smith, sales executive, at GuideStar Data Services in the UK, for their hard work and dedication to UK philanthropy. For our Italian private giving research, we would like to thank Lorena Varalli at Instituto Italiano della Donazione and Sergio Pasquinelli at Instituto per la Ricerca Sociale in Italy.

Lastly, we would like to thank Dilip Ratha, lead economist, and Sanket Mohapatra, economist, of the Migration and Remittance Team at the World Bank for their continued guidance on remittance trends and calculations. Their expertise and contributions to the field of remittance research has been essential to CGP's own report on remittances. We are also grateful to Dr. Ratha for contributing a piece on diaspora bonds to this year's *Index*.

HUDSON INSTITUTE
CENTER FOR GLOBAL PROSPERITY

STAFF

Dr. Carol Adelman, *Director* (1)

Heidi Metcalf Little, *Deputy Director* (2)

Patricia Miller, *Editor* (3)

Jeremiah Norris, *Senior Fellow* (4)

Yulya Spantchak, *Research Fellow* (5)

Kacie Marano, *Executive Assistant* (6)

Tim Ogden, *Consultant* (7)

Charity-Joy Acchiardo (8)

Andrew J Baltes (9)

Patrick Browne (10)

Jason Farrell (11)

Zivile Gedrimaite (12)

Emily Gikow (13)

Anna Greene (14)

Zenah Hasan (15)

Haein Lim (16)

Eimear O'Leary-Barrett (17)

Ai Ghee Ong (18)

Peter J Telaroli (19)

Yan Zhang (20)

PHOTOGRAPH CREDITS